Nick

50 Essentials
for Using
Learning
Technologies

Cambridge Handbooks for Language Teachers

This series, now with over 50 titles, offers practical ideas, techniques and activities for the teaching of English and other languages, providing inspiration for both teachers and trainers.

The Pocket Editions come in a handy, pocket-sized format and are crammed full of tips and ideas from experienced English language teaching professionals, to enrich your teaching practice.

Recent titles in this series:

Nicky Hockly's 50 Essentials for Using Learning Technologies

Nicky Hockly

Consultant and editor: Scott Thornbury

CAMBRIDGE
UNIVERSITY PRESS

University Printing House, Cambridge CB2 8BS, United Kingdom

One Liberty Plaza, 20th Floor, New York, NY 10006, USA

477 Williamstown Road, Port Melbourne, VIC 3207, Australia

314–321, 3rd Floor, Plot 3, Splendor Forum, Jasola District Centre, New Delhi – 110025, India

103 Penang Road, #05–06/07, Visioncrest Commercial, Singapore 238467

Cambridge University Press is part of the University of Cambridge.

It furthers the University's mission by disseminating knowledge in the pursuit of
education, learning and research at the highest international levels of excellence.

www.cambridge.org
Information on this title: www.cambridge.org/9781108932615

© Cambridge University Press 2022

First published 2022

20 19 18 17 16 15 14 13 12 11 10 9 8 7 6 5 4 3 2 1

Printed in Great Britain by CPI Group (UK) Ltd, Croydon CR0 4YY

A catalogue record for this publication is available from the British Library

ISBN 978-1-10893261-5 Paperback
ISBN 978-1-10893264-6 eBook

Contents

Acknowledgements

The authors and publishers acknowledge the following sources of copyright material and are grateful for the permissions granted. While every effort has been made, it has not always been possible to identify the sources of all the material used, or to trace all copyright holders. If any omissions are brought to our notice, we will be happy to include the appropriate acknowledgements on reprinting and in the next update to the digital edition, as applicable.

Text
Chapter 6: Taylor & Francis Group for the adapted text taken from *Digital Literacies* by Gavin Dudeney, Nicola Hockly and Mark Pegrum. Copyright © 2020 Taylor & Francis Group. Reproduced by kind permission of Taylor & Francis Group.

Typeset
Typesetting by QBS Learning.

Why I wrote this book

The extent to which digital technologies have become embedded in our daily lives over the last decade is astounding. Look around you in any public space, and you will inevitably see several people glued to their mobile phones. Our homes, too, are becoming permeated with technology. We get home and watch movies via video streaming services (think Netflix). We ask our personal digital assistants (think Alexa or Google Home) to switch on the lights or to read out a recipe while we cook dinner. The English language classroom has not been immune to the wave of technology sweeping through our lives.

I started work as an English language teacher in 1987, so I have seen a range of technologies come and go in classrooms: tape recorders, video recorders and players, digital cameras, computer labs, CD-ROMs, interactive whiteboards, and more recently mobile devices. Then the COVID-19 pandemic came along, and we witnessed an unprecedented and massive move to online, hybrid and blended teaching in a very short space of time. Even teachers who may have been resistant to using learning technologies in their physical classrooms suddenly gained a considerable amount of teaching online experience, willingly or not. Despite this mass immersion in online teaching tools and technologies, what didn't change – and will not change – is good teaching. Effective teachers don't need the latest technologies or gadgets. They can use whatever technology is available effectively, and if no technology is available, they are still good teachers. They teach well, whether they are online or in the physical classroom. Using technology to *support learning* is the key to teaching well. It is never about the technology; it is always about the teaching and the learning.

As the COVID-19 pandemic made clear, not everyone has unlimited access to technology. The digital divide clearly exists, although it is not necessarily only geographical. A digital divide exists between rural and urban settings, between men and women, between young and old, between cities, between areas in the same city, between schools, and even between classrooms in the same school. It exists between teachers who are confident users of learning technologies and teachers who are not.

I've been lucky enough to work with teachers all over the world, in high and low resource contexts. I've seen teachers with all the technology resources one could imagine deliver less than engaging lessons; I've seen teachers with no technology at all deliver excellent lessons. Nevertheless, it is a fact that access to digital technologies – especially mobile technologies – is easier and more affordable than it has ever been. And since the COVID-19 pandemic, it is also clear that technologies – including mobile devices – can be used to create effective virtual learning spaces when it is not possible for learners to attend physical classes.

Feeling confident with using digital technologies means knowing how to use them effectively to support learning. This also involves understanding the challenges and benefits, as well as knowing how to deal with the issues surrounding the use of learning technologies with learners. This book aims to highlight some of the areas you need to consider in order to use learning technologies effectively. Some of these areas are often not discussed in books that focus exclusively on classroom activities with technology. This is not due to oversight on the part of the writers (I've written a few of these books myself!), but often due to a lack of space. In this book we have space for 50 considerations on how to get the most out of a range of learning technologies, whatever your context.

There are a couple of ways to read this book. You could read it cover to cover, or you may find it useful to read specific sections as and when you need them. You'll notice that I mention a few software programs, apps and websites by name, here and there. We all know that these tend to come and go, so I've tried to choose programs and sites that I think will be around for several more years. However, do keep in mind that the tech landscape can change quickly, and what's popular today may be gone tomorrow. If any of the resources I mention are not around by the time you read this book, simply do a **keyword search** to find a similar tool or website. There's also a Glossary at the end of book, where you can look up terms like *keyword search*, among others, as well as suggestions for further readings, or reference to research, at points. I hope you enjoy the book!

A: Understanding learning technologies

Using learning technologies effectively involves being able to answer some of the big questions. Asking ourselves why we should use them, whether they support learning, and how to choose the best ones, is a good place to start.

1   Do learning technologies work?

> A question that teachers often ask me is, 'Does technology work?' This is an excellent question, but it's not easy to answer.

When teachers ask me if technology works, they are really asking whether learning technologies help their students learn English better. This is probably the most important question to ask. Luckily, there is plenty of research for us to look at, stretching back several decades. The short answer to whether learning technologies help students learn English is, it depends. It's very difficult to make comparisons across research studies that investigate different tools, with different groups of learners and in different contexts. The research studies themselves have different aims, use different teaching materials and tasks, and reflect different research methodologies.

One way to try and answer our question is to look at *meta studies*, that is, papers that review several studies on a topic, and attempt to synthesise the results. Let's look at two meta studies, one on **interactive whiteboards** (**IWBs**) and the other on **Web 2.0** tools. These summaries are necessarily brief, and the interested reader is encouraged to read the originals for more detail.

Study 1 (Higgins, Beauchamp and Miller, 2007): This meta study reviewed the evidence on the effectiveness of IWBs. It focused especially on the impact of IWBs on teaching, and it reviewed the evidence on how IWBs affect learning and achievement for learners. The researchers concluded that, 'although the IWB may alter the way that learning takes place, and that the motivation of teachers and pupils may be increased, yet this may have no significant or measurable impact on achievement' (ibid: 221). This meta study was carried out in 2007, but there has been no significant evidence to contradict these findings to date.

Study 2 (Reinhardt, 2019): This meta study reviewed the research into the use of **blogs, wikis** and social networking sites in English language teaching and learning. The evidence on blogs is largely positive, although certain issues (for example, task design and audience) are key to their successful implementation. The evidence on wikis is mixed: they do not automatically lead to improved learner accuracy, but they can support cooperation between learners. Teacher guidance and feedback, and authentic task design, are key to their success. The research into the effect of using social networking sites to support language learning is also largely positive. Learner community and learner autonomy can be enhanced when these sites are used alongside language classes; however, some learners may be resistant to using social networking sites for learning, or they may resent teacher-imposed activities.

Where does this leave us? Study 1 shows no clear positive results. So, can we say with confidence that IWBs help students learn English better? Based on the evidence, probably not, although they make teachers' jobs easier. On the other hand, Study 2 finds mainly positive evidence for the use of specific Web 2.0 tools, with some caveats. So, can we conclude that blogs, wikis and social networking sites help learners improve their English? The answer in this case is a tentative yes, but keeping in mind the issues and caveats that are highlighted in the meta study.

It's worth bearing in mind that the findings in meta studies may not be generalisable to all contexts. After all, a meta study is a synthesis of lots of smaller studies, and these are often very context-specific. Nevertheless, meta studies are a good place to start if you'd like to get an overview of how effective a specific learning technology is – or isn't. Looking at the research shows us that we need to be critical users of learning technologies, and critical readers of the research. The research shows that some technologies seem to work better than others. Based on this, we need to take an evidence-based approach to choosing and using learning technologies with our own learners.

Higgins, S., Beauchamp, G. and Miller, D. (2007). 'Reviewing the literature on interactive whiteboards', *Learning, Media and Technology*, 32, 3, 213–225.

Reinhardt, J. (2019). 'Social media in second and foreign language teaching and learning: Blogs, wikis, and social networking', *Language Teaching*, 52, 1, 1–39.

2   The shift to online teaching

> The COVID-19 pandemic led to school closures and
> an unprecedented move to online teaching and learning
> across the globe.

UNESCO estimates that at the height of the COVID-19 pandemic in
2020, school closures meant that 1.6 billion children in 195 countries
were out of school. Many schools and higher education institutions
introduced online learning strategies during this time, including the use
of digital textbooks and resources, online learning platforms, live video
classes, and emailing learners work for them to do at home.

But of course, not all countries or learner populations had the necessary
infrastructure or means to move online. If anything, digital inequality
was brought into even starker relief by the pandemic. For many
learners, online learning was simply not an option. In some low resource
contexts with experience of remote non-digital delivery of learning, a
combination of television, radio and take-home paper-based learning
materials was deployed instead. However, some writers pointed out
the pandemic foregrounded the need to provide equitable access to
online learning globally, so that the disadvantaged are not even more
disadvantaged when unable to physically attend school.

In those places where a move online was feasible, online learning
measures had to be introduced with very little preparation, often
overnight. You yourself may suddenly have found yourself teaching
online – possibly from one day to the next! Some writers characterised
this sudden transition as 'remote emergency teaching' rather than
'online teaching' in any principled sense. This was because, in most
cases, teachers received little or no training for the shift to online
teaching. But many teachers managed exceptionally well, showing
extraordinary resilience and resourcefulness, and although they faced
considerable challenges, they also reported triumphs.

Challenges, unsurprisingly, included their school or university's lack of preparedness to move online, and a lack of support. Of course, learners too were unprepared for the sudden move online, and in some cases, simply finding a quiet place in the home from which to teach or learn was a challenge during lockdowns. Parents of young learners often had to juggle home-schooling with teleworking, and not all families had access to sufficient hardware. But there were many triumphs. For example, despite a very steep learning curve for some teachers, many soon became proficient at delivering live classes via video-conferencing. Teachers reported that managing young learner classes was often easier online, and that many shy learners blossomed, contributing much more in virtual breakout rooms than they had ever done in the physical classroom. A further positive to emerge was that teachers were able to experiment, learn and grow professionally – I heard many reports from English language teachers that although challenging, the move online provided them with a tremendous professional development opportunity. At the time of writing this book (2021), the dust has not yet settled on the COVID-19 pandemic, and the long term effects on English language teaching remain to be seen. What has emerged though, is that schools and universities are looking at online and blended learning more seriously than before. Through personal experience, teachers have realised that online learning doesn't have to replace the bricks and mortar classroom, but it can enhance and support what we do in the classroom, and when necessary, entirely replace it.

Overall, there has been a global awakening to the potential and challenges of digital and online learning. The COVID-19 epidemic may have been unprecedented in its effect on education globally, but localised school shutdowns due to epidemics, natural disasters, political turmoil or war are, sadly, nothing new. More than ever before, governments are aware that investment in the infrastructure, resources, teacher training, and learner and parental support for effective online learning are needed to avoid the loss of educational opportunity for learners in times of such crises. Online learning in ELT has, it seems, become mainstream.

3 Teaching with technology in low resource contexts

The technologies used to support English language learning in low resource contexts are often a mix of older established technologies such as radio and television, and more recent mobile-based technologies such as group messaging apps.

The *digital divide* is often cited as a barrier to the use of technologies in low resource contexts. The digital divide is most commonly understood as the division between developed countries, who, it is argued, have good access to digital technologies, and developing countries who do not. But the digital divide can exist *within* countries, where those living in urban areas may have good access to technologies, while those living in remote and rural areas may not. It can exist within individual classrooms, where some learners may have access to computers or the internet at home, while others may not. A digital divide can also exist based on gender, age, and levels of education and income – even in high resource contexts. We may see digital divides among teachers, based on skill and access to training, where some teachers may have the necessary skills to use digital technologies to support their learners' learning more effectively than others. This more nuanced understanding of the digital divide reminds us that teachers in high resource contexts may find themselves teaching in resource-poor schools or classrooms; teachers in low resource contexts may find themselves teaching in high resource urban environments.

The key to the effective use of learning technologies in low resource contexts centres around the use of the appropriate technologies for that context, the cultural appropriacy of materials and teaching/learning approaches, cost-effectiveness, and sustainability. This sounds like a tall order. It can be useful to look outside the field of ELT for effective educational projects that manage to achieve this. In my view, one particularly effective and interesting initiative that ticks all of these boxes is an online training course developed by MIT (the Massachusetts Institute of Technology) and a South African NGO called 'Grassroot'. The online training course aimed to develop leadership skills for community organisers, but course delivery had to be low tech, given high data costs in South Africa and a significant rural/urban digital divide. The project team developed an approach that delivered real time lessons/tasks via the group messaging app WhatsApp, during which facilitators and participants interacted by using text, images/photos, emoticons, and audio notes. This project took advantage of technologies that course participants already had (in this case, WhatsApp and **feature phones**), and designed effective, engaging and media rich learning tasks around that. Within the field of ELT, there have been projects to teach English in low resource contexts by sending regular SMS or instant group messages to learners, with items of vocabulary or idioms for them to learn.

English language teachers in low resource contexts can take ideas and inspiration from such projects. If your learners already use group messaging apps such as WhatsApp, Telegram or similar, you can set regular short language-related tasks for them to complete in the messaging app. For example, you could set your learners a weekly audio dictation via an audio or voice note. Or you could choose a lexical set, and ask learners to each post a photo and description of an item related to the lexical set to the group. Design short simple tasks that use the full range of features of a messaging app, and that can be carried out on a **feature phone**, rather than a smartphone. You could hold regular WhatsApp/Telegram classes in real time, for example, for an hour a week, in which learners can discuss a topic via text or voice note messages.

4 Choosing appropriate learning technologies

> If you plan to use learning technologies with your learners, it's important to choose wisely and well. There is no point in using technology for its own sake. Technology needs to be integrated into teaching and learning in a *principled* way.

Technology needs to bring something to the language learning experience, not just in individual lessons (whether online or in the physical classroom), but throughout the course. With so many tools and technologies available, many of them for free, teachers can feel overwhelmed by choice. Here are four key areas to consider, to help you decide whether a certain technology or tool is useful or not.

1 **Availability and appropriacy**: What technologies are already available to you and your learners (e.g. mobile phones; internet access at school and at home, etc.)? What technologies are appropriate for the context and age of your learners? For example, if you'd like your learners to use their mobile devices to support their language learning, expensive data plans may make their use for homework or self-study unrealistic; the use of mobile phones in the classroom may be restricted in your school; parents may be resistant to the use of mobiles with younger learners because they do not see them as serious study tools; the content of a learning app you'd like your learners to use may not be culturally appropriate. What is *available* is not necessarily *appropriate*, so this is the first area to consider.

2 **Value for learning**: How does your chosen technology or tool support and enhance your students' learning? How does it support learning outcomes? Learning outcomes may relate to language skills (e.g. vocabulary, grammar, pronunciation and the four skills), but they can also include important non-linguistic skills (e.g. digital literacies, critical thinking, creativity, intercultural communication, etc.). Also, ask yourself what added value the technology or tool

brings to the activity. For example, does it increase your learners' motivation and engagement with the learning materials? If so, will they spend more time working with the materials out of school? Motivation and engagement, which can lead to additional exposure to the language, can improve learning outcomes too.

3   **Time and effort**: How long will it take for you and your learners to learn how to use a certain tool or technology effectively? How much effort is involved? Some tools are easy to set up and use (e.g. quiz apps), but others can take much more time and planning (e.g. a **blog** or a **VLE**). However, it's not necessarily a case of the simpler the better. You need to consider how long you and your learners will actually use the tool for, both in and out of class. Let's take a blog as an example of a slightly more complex tool. It may take some time to set up a class blog, and it may take careful planning and time for your learners to use it regularly, but this is a tool that you can use over a period of time (e.g. a term or semester), and with appropriate tasks, your learners can produce a significant amount of writing and multimedia. In this particular case, the time and effort involved in setting up the tool, teaching your learners how to use it, and designing appropriate tasks, can be worth it.

4   **Digital skills**: What digital literacy skills do you and your learners need to be able to use the technology or tool effectively? These skills may be technological (e.g. how to create a blog post or a Word document; how to add an image or a **hyperlink** to a document), but they can also be skills related to the appropriate use of technologies in social contexts (see **6**). For example, your learners may know how to add an online image to a blog post, but do they know that they need to respect copyright, and that they can use Creative Commons licensed images (see **35**)? Do they know about various types of plagiarism, how to avoid it, and how to attribute their online sources correctly (see **36**)?

Using learning technologies to support special educational needs (SEN)

Assistive technologies can help learners with a range of special educational needs in the English language classroom. Let's examine how.

There are different terms used to talk about learners with unique learning needs. You may have come across the term *special educational needs*, or SEN for short. You may also have come across the term *neurodiversity*. Neurodiversity is often used to refer to those learners who may face cognitive or learning challenges such as **dyslexia** or autism, behavioural challenges like ADHD (attention deficit hyperactivity disorder), or social or emotional difficulties. Some learners may face physical challenges such as sight or hearing impairment, or restricted movement and limited motor skills; in these cases, the term SEN may be considered more appropriate. In this chapter I use the term SEN because technology can provide effective support for learners with a range of needs, from cognitive, emotional and behavioural to physical.

Many classrooms today support inclusive practices. This means that learners with special educational needs are included in classrooms rather than being taught in separate classes or schools. Within inclusive classrooms, mobile technologies and especially tablet computers, have been enthusiastically taken up by teachers working with SEN learners because of their assistive features. For example, a written text in English can be listened to by activating a tablet's text to speech capability. This provides support for dyslexic learners, who may find the act of reading challenging; it can also provide audio access to written text for the partially sighted or blind. Tablets also have speech to text capability; in this case, a learner with partial or full hearing impairment can have audio content transcribed into text, for example, by activating closed captions (subtitles) on videos. Learners can also change the font and size of subtitles for ease of viewing. Other assistive features for learners with hearing impairment include a mono (rather than the default stereo) option in sound settings, and hearing aids can connect to some tablets via Bluetooth.

For learners with motor skills challenges like **dyspraxia,** tactile screen settings can be changed from swipe movements to tapping movements, which are easier to control; also, the screen display on mobile devices can be locked into one position so that screen movement for these learners is reduced.

Finally, some tablets include an assistive touch feature that allows teachers to guide learners around the screen as they read.

Unsurprisingly, there is also a wide range of educational apps available for SEN learners, including those learning a second or foreign language. For example, for dyslexic learners, there are writing apps that can help them learn to spell letters by tracing them on a touch screen. SEN learners with autism or behavioural challenges can benefit from more sophisticated apps that enable teachers to create video scenarios in order to help these learners develop empathy and social skills.

There is a substantial body of research into the effectiveness of assistive technologies in general education. The results are promising, with research suggesting that the **multimodal** and tactile qualities of tablets can improve communication and literacy development for autistic learners in the classroom, as well as increase engagement, develop academic and communicative skills, and improve social interaction. There is considerably less research into SEN learners and English language learning, although this will hopefully change as inclusive approaches to English language learning become more widespread. Nevertheless, one study with seven to eight years old SEN learners in the USA found that tablet-based multimodal English language learning material enabled these learners to work more independently and increased their engagement. However, engagement declined in the longer term, possibly due to the repetitive nature of the learning materials and activities. As with any learning materials, those delivered with the aid of assistive technologies also need to be relevant and interesting to keep learners engaged.

6 Digital literacies

> Digital literacies are the technology skills and social practices needed to use digital technologies appropriately and effectively.

Whenever I give a training session about digital literacies to language teachers, I first ask them what they think the term means. Often, the first definition that jumps into people's minds is technology skills. But digital literacies are much more than simply knowing how to use technologies from a technical perspective. So what are they? Let's look at an example.

Imagine that you ask a group of university students to write an essay about a topic that they need to research online. You ask them to write their essays in a word processing program, with links to online sources to back up their arguments, and to include images to illustrate their texts. Your learners probably know how to create a word-processed document, how to create **hyperlink**s to their online sources, and how to find online images and insert these into their texts. This is what we can call basic *technological literacy*. But do the learners know how to search effectively for online sources (search literacy), and then evaluate whether these online sources are reliable (information literacy)? Research suggests that they don't (Wineburg et al., 2016). And although the learners may know how to include hyperlinks in their texts, have they considered how many hyperlinks to include and what effect over-hyperlinking has on the reader? Too many hyperlinks in a text can hinder comprehension and retention of information, so judicious hyperlinking is an important part of hypertext literacy. And what about the use of images in their texts? Have the learners inserted copyright protected images, or have they used freely available Creative Commons licensed images (see **35**) – and attributed these images correctly (**multimodal** literacy)? As this example shows, even a relatively straightforward digital task like writing an essay in a word processing program requires learners to draw on several digital literacies.

To help unpack the idea of digital literacies, I find it useful to think of them within four different areas or foci (Dudeney, Hockly and Pegrum, 2013; Pegrum, Hockly and Dudeney, 2022).

- The first focus includes literacies that focus on *communication*. Here we find hypertext and multimodal literacy as described in the example above, where text and images are used to communicate information, among others.
- The second focus is around *information*, such as the search and information literacies described above, among others.
- The third focus includes digital literacies that are concerned with *collaboration*. Here we find personal literacy (knowing how to shape and protect your online identity), and intercultural literacy (knowing how to communicate effectively across cultures in the digital sphere), among others.
- Finally, the fourth focus is around *(re)design*, and includes remix literacy, a creative process that involves modifying and adapting existing **digital artefact**s to create new ones. We also find a raft of critical literacies, including critical philosophical literacy (for example, asking what our increasing dependence on smart devices, robots and AI might mean for the future), among others.

Of course, a close look at all of the digital literacies – and how we can support our learners in developing them in our English language classes – is simply not possible here. But the example of asking your learners to write an essay, as described earlier, might be a good way to start raising their awareness of certain essential digital literacies.

Dudeney, G., Hockly, N. and Pegrum, M. (2013). *Digital Literacies*. London: Routledge.

Pegrum, M., Hockly, N. and Dudeney, G. (2022). *Digital Literacies: second edition*. London: Routledge.

Wineburg, S., McGrew, S., Breakstone, J. and Ortega, T. (2016). *Evaluating Information: The Cornerstone of Civic Online Reasoning*. Stanford Digital Repository. Available at: http://purl.stanford.edu/fv751yt5934

Screen time

> Children of all ages seem to spend a lot of time staring at the screens of digital devices. Many parents and teachers are asking themselves, 'How much screen time should children be exposed to?'

With greater access to mobile devices, children have more screen time at home than previously, when only television was available. Outside of school, the amount of time that children spend looking at screens depends on their age and context. For example, two- to four-year-olds in the USA can spend over two hours a day looking at screens on average. This can increase to around four hours a day by the age of seven. As children get older, they spend more time looking at screens, but less of that time is spent with educational content. And teenagers aged 13 and over can spend up to an astounding seven to nine hours a day on their phones.

Studies into the effects of screen time on children have mixed results. Some studies have found links between excessive screen time and issues such as expressive language delay, inattention, sleep deprivation, depression and obesity. Other studies highlight that it is *how* screens are used that is the important factor, not just the amount of time spent on them. For example, the judicious use of social networks can lead to increased social interaction and a sense of connection; physical activity can be encouraged in mobile games like Pokémon Go, or with devices like the Nintendo Wii.

As digital technologies are increasingly present in schools, children's screen time increases. Nevertheless, educators generally agree that it is important for children to acquire technology skills and to develop their digital literacies, and that primary and secondary schools are the best places to develop these. There is also research showing that when some digital technologies are integrated into classroom activities in a pedagogically sound manner, they can support language learning (see **1**). This presents us with a bit of a conundrum. Should we or shouldn't we use digital technologies in the classroom, if our learners are already exposed to so much screen time out of school? The answer is not to ban digital technologies from the classroom, but rather to ensure that they are used in an age-appropriate and judicious manner. For example, the World Health Organization suggests no more than one hour of screen time a day for two- to five-year-olds. Teachers of very young learners already know that English language learning activities should include plenty of physical movement, singing, drawing and play, etc., and that activities with digital technologies should be limited. Some very young learner teachers prefer to have completely digital free classrooms, and this is fine. However, from primary school onwards, digital technologies are present in many contexts. In order to ensure a judicious use of these technologies, the aims of digital activities need to be carefully considered, with a clear understanding of what they bring to the learning process. Schools may also want to discuss age-appropriate amounts of screen time with parents, who may be unaware of WHO guidelines. Tips shared with parents might include how to use apps that limit the amount of time children can use a particular digital device in the home, for example.

For teachers of all age groups, it's important that screen time at school is balanced with other activities, including physical activities. It's also important that quality educational content is used on digital devices in schools and that digital tasks are designed to maximise language learning. Digital devices are here to stay, and they need to be used in effective and appropriate ways in schools. Taking screen time into account is an important part of this.

B: Teaching and learning approaches

Technologies and the internet provide a range of ways for teachers to teach – and for learners to learn – that goes well beyond the physical classroom. Combining physical and virtual spaces to support learning is increasingly common, so teachers may need to adapt their traditional roles and teaching approaches.

Informal online language learning

From the early days of the internet, learners have been able to learn independently online. These days, learners are likely to use language learning apps and/or social networking to improve their English outside the classroom.

When talking about online learning, we need to start by clarifying our terminology. Terms like *e-learning*, *distance learning*, *remote learning* and *web-enhanced learning* are used with varying degrees of frequency to refer to essentially the same phenomenon – that of learning online, either synchronously (in real time) and/or asynchronously (time independent). Add to that terms like *blended*, *hybrid* or *mixed* learning, and teachers can be forgiven for feeling a little confused! Although we will examine each of these modalities of learning later in this book, we start with learning 100 percent online, with no face-to-face component, and in *informal* settings. By this I mean learners who study online independently of teachers and classrooms (virtual or physical), in an ad hoc and unstructured fashion in their own time, and by setting their own learning agendas, whether consciously or not. I use the umbrella term *online learning* because it's broad enough to include a variety of digital learning options, including language learning apps and social networking, the focus of this chapter.

Currently popular language learning apps include Duolingo, Busuu and Babbel, aimed at adult learners. These types of apps essentially adopt a **behaviourist approach** to language learning, with automated language activities delivered via an engaging mobile interface. In some apps, learners can score points by completing activities and games, reflecting a **gamification** approach that some learners find motivating; other apps incorporate more recent technologies such as augmented reality (see **43**), but the approach to learning remains firmly traditional, with memorisation and repetition at the heart of the learning approach. Memorisation and repetition are important in language learning of course, and the spaced repetition that these apps provide can be highly effective for the learning of new vocabulary.

But unsurprisingly, where these apps tend to fall short is in providing opportunities for meaningful interaction with others, an essential component of language learning. Other online language learning providers have stepped in to fill this need though, and we find language exchange apps such as Tandem, which offers users a chance to interact with others in the language of their choice via text, audio and/or video. Learners can also engage in meaningful interaction in social networking sites like Facebook, Instagram and Twitter, etc.; indeed, there is a growing body of research that attests to the incidental learning that can take place when learners social network in English (see Reinhardt, 2019). Studies have also found that learners' motivation can increase, and if a class social networking site is set up, a stronger and closer group dynamic can be fostered (see Kelley, 2010).

Despite their limitations, language learning apps can provide useful additional language practice. Research shows that these apps have a high dropout rate because of the self-discipline required to use them over the long-term, but there is no harm in showing your learners what apps are available and inviting them to choose and try one out over a period of a few weeks or a month – if they would like to. The trick is to then integrate this into the classroom, by regularly inviting learners to share in class what they have learned in their chosen app, what they like about it, and what they find less effective. This regular sharing might encourage a more reluctant learner to try out an app. Even if learners get bored with an app and move to another, or stop entirely, any extra engagement with language learning, and being exposed to English outside the classroom is a good thing. It may also help your learners develop some autonomy and self-reliance in language learning. Supporting learners in gaining additional exposure to English, and promoting learner independence, are both worthwhile goals for any teacher.

Kelley, J. A. (2010). 'Social network sites and the ideal L2 self: Using Myspace in a Chinese EFL class', *The JALT CALL Journal*, 6.1, 17–33.

Reinhardt, J. (2019). 'Social media in second and foreign language teaching and learning: Blogs, wikis, and social networking', *Language Teaching*, 52, 1, 1–39.

> Whereas informal online language learning is unstructured and often ad hoc, formal online language learning implies learners taking part in more structured learning activities, usually as part of a prepared course of study.

Formal courses will usually include a focus on all four language skills (reading, writing, listening, and speaking), as well as on grammar and vocabulary. Based on approaches found in contemporary communicative language teaching coursebooks, often with themed units and an integrated skills approach, formal online language learning may include synchronous teacher-led online lessons in a video-conferencing platform; it will also usually include asynchronous work such as reading or viewing online content and responding to that content via quizzes and/or online discussions in a **virtual learning environment (VLE)**. Online language courses offered by schools and universities, or real-time online classes with a private online teacher, can both be considered formal opportunities for online learning; at the very least they require learners to invest regular chunks of time (and often money) over a period of time, and they are usually led by teachers. Massive open online courses for learning languages (LMOOCs) can also be considered examples of formal online learning. **MOOCs** typically need learners to take responsibility for their own learning, are not dependent on teachers being present, and can be cost free.

Of course, the big question is: does formal online language learning work? In other words, is it possible to actually learn a language fully online? Much early research into fully online language learning centred around the extent to which the online mode was better or worse than the face-to-face mode, with the high dropout rates on online courses, and particularly on MOOCs, often cited as evidence of them being 'worse'. However, with badly designed online courses being compared to frequently more engaging face-to-face courses, it soon became evident that this was not the best research question. Whether an online course is more or less effective than a face-to-face equivalent rests on a multitude of factors, not on the delivery mode alone. Factors include effective course and task design; learners' preferences, motivation and expectations; teacher skills (including being trained in online teaching); learner support; and – in the case of an online language course – to what extent the course actually provides opportunities for language learning, including real-time spoken interaction.

Although 100 percent online language schools have existed since at least the mid-1990s, the COVID-19 pandemic saw massive amounts of teaching, including formal language courses, move fully online. In some cases, these online learning experiences were effective and successful; in other cases they were less effective. All of the factors mentioned above (i.e. course design, learner preferences and support, teachers' skills, etc.) came into play, so varying degrees of success with online learning was inevitable. If anything, the COVID-19 experience of moving formal language learning courses online for several months at a time, highlighted the need for teachers to be prepared and trained, for learners to have access to the necessary infrastructure and resources, and for online tasks and courses to be effectively designed. When these three elements (teachers, learners and learning content) are optimally aligned, online learning can indeed be effective.

However, it can take a considerable investment of time and money to design a well-structured online language course with motivating tasks, multimedia, opportunities for learner-learner interaction, and an engaging platform for delivery. In my experience of designing online language learning materials for schools, it can take up to eight hours of development time to create one hour of online learning materials and tasks. If multimedia like audio and video needs to be developed from scratch, it can take longer. Mindful of this, some schools prefer to offer off-the-shelf online learning materials to their learners, designed by online language learning providers or ELT publishers, rather than develop this content themselves. Whichever approach is taken, it is clear that providing online and blended learning options for learners is an important part of future-proofing for any ELT institution.

Teaching online requires balancing four overlapping areas: hardware, software, liveware and courseware. Let's explore what each of these is, and how they can be integrated to support effective online teaching.

I find it useful to think of teaching online as involving four key areas. First, there is the *hardware*, which may be a computer or digital device, and should include a microphone and speakers (or preferably a headset for better audio quality), a webcam, and a reliable internet connection. Then there is the *software*. This may be a **virtual learning environment** (**VLE**) and/or video-conferencing platform, a **blog** or **wiki** or social networking platform, and any other programs through which your online course is delivered. Thirdly, there is the *liveware* or the human element, that is, the teacher and learners; this is also sometimes referred to as the *wetware*, perhaps not the most attractive of terms! Finally, there is the *courseware* – that is, the course content that you plan to teach, and the online tasks that you create to do so.

Teaching online means integrating and balancing these areas. For example, if you are teaching a writing class online, you are going to need a platform that enables your learners to write, and to respond to each other's writing. In this case, a VLE with forum discussions, a class and/or individual blogs, or even a social networking site, are all possible software choices. Which is the best choice? Here is where we need to think about the liveware, or the learners. How old are they? What sort of writing do they need to learn? Teaching academic writing to university students is very different to teaching younger teenagers writing, and your choice of platform should reflect this difference. A VLE or blog is well suited to the long-form writing needed for English for Academic Purposes (EAP), whereas a social networking tool that lends itself to shorter social forms of writing may be more effective with teenagers. Remember, however, that using social networking tools with younger learners means paying close attention to e-safety and gaining parental permission (see 33); in this case, matching software, liveware and courseware requires considerations that go beyond just choosing the best technology for the job.

Although there is a tendency in online learning to think that a VLE (such as Moodle, Canvas or Blackboard) is the best choice, as we've seen above, this is not necessarily true. A VLE is perhaps the most complete solution in that is allows you to host all of your course content (documents, images, audio, video) easily in one place, and to integrate tools for communication into tasks (wikis, blogs, forums), as well as offering robust learner tracking and grading. Most VLEs will offer all of these features, but the real question is – do you really need a VLE?

If you are teaching a conversation class online, your platform of choice is likely to be a video-conferencing tool with breakout rooms, so that you can then use them to give your learners plenty of opportunities to practise their speaking in pairs and small groups. Speaking practice can be supported with asynchronous work in a VLE, but it might be more effective to use simpler tools such as Google Classroom, or even just a Google Doc, where your learners can carry out asynchronous work before or after your online class, and even during the live class.

I have been training teachers in how to teach online for over two decades, and although there is a tendency to focus initially on the hardware and software, with teachers often feeling challenged by the technology, it's the liveware that's essential. As with face-to-face teaching, creating a good rapport with learners online is important and can directly impact your learners' motivation. Online rapport can also be fostered through good task design, where tasks include plenty of personalisation and learners are encouraged to share and communicate with each other.

Teaching online via video-conferencing has become increasingly common over the last few years. It can, however, throw up some challenges for teachers.

Teaching via video-conferencing remained a minority endeavour until the COVID-19 epidemic led to worldwide school closures and a massive shift to online teaching (see **2**). The upshot of this was that many teachers suddenly gained experience of teaching English live online, whereas prior to March 2020, relatively few had done so. I was involved in a great deal of training at this time, and this enabled me to work closely with teachers grappling with several issues when teaching via video-conferencing. These issues remain important to keep in mind when teaching live online, no matter how much experience you may have.

The first challenge is to avoid the tendency to lecture learners about language. Video-conferencing can very easily become a teacher-led tool. The webcam can sometimes have a spotlight effect, with the teacher feeling that she has to fill the silence by talking, leaving learners as passive onlookers who frequently have their own webcams turned off. Learning to avoid excessive teacher talk by designing communicative language tasks that encourage learners to talk in pairs and small groups, in breakout rooms where possible, is an important first step for teachers wanting to move towards a less teacher-centric approach. Pair and small group work in breakout rooms has the added advantage of enabling learners to use their webcams without feeling threatened by appearing in front of the whole group. Having the teacher *and* learners use their webcams in a live online class is an important part of establishing a group dynamic and creating rapport, so the use of webcams needs to be encouraged as much as possible. In some cases, however, it may not be culturally appropriate for learners to appear on camera; in other cases, limited bandwidth may mean that learners are simply unable to use their webcams. Instead, learners can choose a profile image or icon that they feel represents them, and use audio only. In these cases, learners can share with their online classmates why they chose a particular image or icon, in the first live online class. With learners under the age of 18, having webcams turned on can be part of the online class rules, with parents informed of these, and contacted when learners claim that their webcams don't work. For adults, the use of webcams (when, why, for how long) can be negotiated, and introduced slowly via breakout room activities for reluctant groups.

One of my favourite breakout room activities, that can be carried out in pairs early on in a course, and that requires the use of learners' webcams, is to ask each learner to share an object that has sentimental value for them with the class. This kind of simple personalised task allows for plenty of student talking time, it encourages group bonding *and* it gets learners using their webcams in a meaningful way.

The chatbox is another helpful feature of video-conferencing platforms. It can be used for teacher-learner interaction, and also for correction, feedback, praise, the sharing of links, etc. One of my favourite closing activities in live classes gets learners to complete sentence stems in the chatbox, starting with *One thing ...* (e.g. *One thing I'm going to do after class is ...* ; *One thing I've learned today is ...* etc.).

Finally, most platforms include a whiteboard where teachers and learners can write, type or draw. Some teachers also like to use a small portable whiteboard, on which to write up incidental vocabulary, to draw diagrams or timelines to illustrate a point, or to keep scores during games. A portable whiteboard can be held up to the camera to support an off-the-cuff explanation, and it's often quicker to use than activating the built-in whiteboard.

> **Blended learning is an umbrella term that most commonly refers to some combination of in-class or face-to-face learning and online learning.**

Learners increasingly expect to be able to fit learning English into their own busy lives and working schedules. This is particularly true of university students, and adults who are busy professionals, and as we have seen in previous chapters, there is a wealth of informal online learning options that learners can engage in, if they so choose. For those learners who expect some degree of choice and flexibility over where, how and when they learn, but want this to form part of a formal or structured course of study, blended learning makes sense. Blended learning options are also increasingly common with learners under the age of 18. Like hybrid teaching (see **13**), blended learning options were brought into the educational mainstream on a large scale due to the COVID-19 pandemic; in some institutions, blended learning options came to stay.

There is no one right blend. The amount of face-to-face instruction versus online instruction can vary widely, and will depend on your teaching context, the needs and expectations of your learners, the resources you have available, and the content and design of your course, to name just a few factors. Let's look at a number of possible blended learning scenarios.

1   A business English teacher offers her learners three hours of classes a week. Because her learners are busy professionals, they cannot come to more than one hour per week of physical class time. So she offers her learners an additional two hours per week of online work. One of those hours takes place via a live video-conferencing session; the other hour requires her learners to complete asynchronous tasks, individually, in pairs, and/or in small groups via a **VLE**.
2   A language school in the UK offers intensive 25-hour-per-week summer courses to international students of all ages. After they leave the UK, they complete an additional ten hours of online work over several weeks.

3   A secondary school teacher has her learners for two hours of class a week in school. She runs a synchronous WhatsApp lesson once a week for 45 minutes, with her learners completing short tasks via text and audio in real time.

4   A primary school teacher meets her learners for three hours a week of face-to-face EFL classes. For homework, she regularly sets tasks using a range online tools, such as creating online slides, creating mobile phone video or audio clips in English, and posting to the class **blog** or **wiki**.

Scenario 4 is often where teachers start experimenting with blended learning, if they have a choice.

The best way to start introducing a blend of face-to-face and online into your teaching, is to start small, preferably with one class, and offering as little as ten percent of classroom work online, possibly simply as an extra like in scenario 4 above. Once you and your learners gain confidence with the tools and online work, you can build more online components into your course.

Blended learning is most effective when it is carefully planned, with the face-to-face and online components complementing and extending each other. Start with an overview of your syllabus or coursebook, and decide which elements to offer online, and which to offer in the physical classroom. Mapping your coursebook syllabus for blended delivery over an entire month or term can help ensure continuity and the effective integration of the various parts.

Using a blended model does not necessarily require expensive technologies, or for you to work in a high resource context. For example, email or group messaging apps like Telegram or WhatsApp are possible low tech alternatives. However, in a fully blended course, it makes sense to try and keep your learners' tasks and work in one place online, such as in a class wiki, a blog or in a VLE. Whatever tool you use for the blended part of your course, start small, try it out, get feedback from your learners, and then adjust your task types and online delivery tools in the light of this.

Hybrid teaching and learning involves some learners being physically present in the classroom, while others attend the class online at the same time, via a video-conferencing platform.

Frequently used as another term for *blended learning* (see **12**), hybrid teaching and learning has become synonymous in ELT with teaching in the physical classroom *and* in the online space at the same time. Although this approach has been around since at least the early 2000s, the COVID-19 pandemic saw many teachers teaching in socially distanced classrooms, where, due to limited classroom space or self-isolation, some learners attended the physical classroom, and others attended class online via video-conferencing, simultaneously. Other terms for hybrid learning include *blended synchronous learning*, and *HyFlex* (hybrid flexible) learning, although this latter option allows learners to choose between the physical classroom, the synchronous online classroom, *and* an asynchronous mode of learning.

As teachers quickly discover, there are a number of challenges associated with teaching in hybrid mode, borne out by research (see the reference below). These challenges include a) the logistics of teaching in a physical and virtual space simultaneously; and b) creating effective tasks for learners in this dual mode of teaching. Let's look at each of these challenges in turn.

First, the logistics. The learners in the virtual space (ideally a video-conferencing platform) need to be able to see and hear the teacher, their virtual classmates, and their in-class classmates. The learners in the physical classroom can easily see and hear the physically present teacher, but they also need to see and hear their online peers. The teacher needs to see and hear *both* groups of learners. This requires careful thinking through of logistics and equipment. The teacher can bring the online learners into the physical classroom by projecting the video-conferencing platform onto the whiteboard; a laptop/computer is needed for this. At the same time, the laptop/computer webcam needs to be aimed at the teacher *and* the in-class learners, so that the online learners can see them. Speakers are needed, to broadcast the online learners into the classroom at times; and an external microphone that the teacher can pass around to the in-class learners is also needed, so that the online learners can hear their in-class peers. The teacher also needs to wear a headset with microphone, to be able to clearly hear the online learners, and to address them at the same time as the in-class learners. Good in-class audio is essential for the online learners; if they can't hear, they will switch off – possibly in both senses of the word!

Second, the tasks. Research (see the reference below) shows that unless the online learners are deliberately integrated into the physical classroom, they feel isolated and soon disengage. Tasks that require pair work between one physically present learner and one online learner are possible, but require additional equipment (e.g. each in-class learner needs a laptop or mobile device with a headset to be able to communicate with their online partner). Some teachers prefer to set tasks that have their learners work in class-only pairs and groups, and in online-only pairs and groups. The reporting back stage of these tasks then involves each pair or group reporting to the whole class, both physical and virtual, via the speakers and/or external microphone. However pair and group work are set up, it's important for teachers to include communicative tasks in hybrid classes, to ensure that learners are engaged and practising the language, regardless of whether they are physically present or online.

The sudden increase in hybrid teaching due to the COVID-19 pandemic gave schools and institutions a taste of another blended learning model to offer their learners. When done well, it can be an effective model, and may suit some adult learners; as such, it is an option well worth considering in terms of the flexibility it can offer learners.

Bower, M., Dalgarno, B., Kennedy, G. E., Lee, M. J. W. and Kenney, J. (2015). 'Design and implementation factors in blended synchronous learning environments: Outcomes from a cross-case analysis', *Computers and Education*, 86: 1–17.

The flipped classroom 14

The term *flipped learning* has become a bit of a buzzword in ELT over the last decade. But what is flipped learning, what does the flipped classroom look like, and most importantly – how does it support language learning?

The basic idea behind the flipped classroom is that learners do essential preparation work online before coming to class. Rather than a teacher standing in front of the class lecturing about a language point, learners can watch an online video about it at home, as many times as necessary, and in their own time. The video may have been prepared by the teacher herself, or by others. The video doesn't need to be a lecture on a language point though! It might include slides, images, cartoons, etc., and it presents the language point to learners in a clear and engaging way, with plenty of examples. Learners can then do some online grammatical exercises to practise the basics of the language point. Learners come to class ready to do more challenging work in the classroom, or to activate newly-acquired knowledge, with the teacher there to support them. Classroom work could involve learners working in pairs creating and acting out dialogues that use the language point in real life scenarios. Or it could involve a role play, or a discussion activity. The point is that learners get the chance to try *using* the language in class, in more challenging speaking activities. Producing language in communicative situations is an essential part of language learning. But when most of the time in class is spent on the teacher explaining language and learners doing mechanical language activities, there is often not enough time for this vital component of a class. By flipping the classroom, more time is available in class for learners to actually use the language, at least in theory.

Technology is not necessary to flip your classroom, but it can certainly enhance the experience for your learners. For example, you can use screen recording software like Camtasia to record a slide-based language presentation, or you could even record yourself giving a language presentation in front of a whiteboard. You can also point your learners to materials that are already available online (TED Talks and YouTube videos are two options popular with teachers). Tools like EdPuzzle enable you to add quiz questions to ready-made videos, which your learners can view before coming to class. However, it's important to remember that the flipped classroom is not about technology. It's about pedagogy. It requires a change in perception of your role from explainer of language to facilitator of learning.

There are some potential challenges with the flipped classroom. For example, not all teachers take advantage of the classroom time freed up by the flipped approach to engage their learners in communicative activities. And what if your learners don't do the pre-class work at home, and then come to class unprepared? What the teacher *shouldn't* do is explain the language point from the beginning! That immediately undermines the need for learners to prepare in advance. Instead, let the unprepared learners work on your planned communicative activities with prepared learners and they will soon see the need to do the pre-class work. Another option is to include the completion of pre-class language exercises in overall course assessment. But some learners may not be mature enough for the flipped classroom, or it may be an approach that does not fit with your educational context. It's important to first discuss the rationale of a flipped classroom approach with your learners, so that they understand how having the chance to communicate in class will improve their English. Also, make sure the preparation work you ask your learners to do is interesting and engaging. Hours of video language lectures are unlikely to motivate your learners to do pre-class work!

Learning with mobile devices – often referred to as *mobile* or *m-learning* – has become increasingly accepted in ELT, as both teachers and learners realise it has the potential to engage learners inside the classroom, and to extend learning beyond the classroom.

The use of handheld devices (such as **feature phones**, smartphones and tablets) is deeply embedded in our personal lives. In low resource contexts where technology is scarce and data costs are relatively high, learners are more likely to have access to a mobile device than to any other form of technology. Most mobile devices have a range of built-in features that can be used to support English language learning, either in and/or outside the classroom. For example:

- Camera: learners can use their mobile devices to take photos outside of school, and then bring these photos to class in order to stimulate discussion. For example, for homework ask your learners to take two or three photos related to the current theme in your coursebook, and then to compare and discuss their photos in class. If mobile devices are banned in your school, your learners can email you their photos, and you can share them on slides in class. This is just one example of how learners' out-of-class photos can act as a springboard for speaking in class.
- Audio: learners can record themselves taking part in pair work speaking activities in class, and then review their conversations, noting down areas for improvement. They can do the same out of class, with individual speaking activities. Out of class, learners can record the sounds of their neighbourhood to share and discuss in class, or they can listen to podcasts in their own time (see **19**).
- Video: learners can video record themselves giving presentations or taking part in role plays in class. As with audio recordings, learners can be encouraged to review and analyse their performance of such

class-based tasks. Of course learners can use their mobile devices to view videos in or out of class as well.

- Text: learners can take short dictations in the notes function on their phones, or share messages (including multimedia) in a class social network. The small screen size and keyboards of most mobile devices mean that they are better suited to short texts, whether produced or read by learners.
- Apps: there are plenty of vocabulary and grammar apps available for English learners, as well as apps that provide skills practice. Learners often find dictionary and translation apps (see **41**) particularly helpful.

For teachers working in schools that ban mobile devices in the classroom, mobile-based activities can be integrated into out-of-class work, especially if you use a social network like WhatsApp, Telegram, Instagram or Facebook with your learners (with the necessary permissions in place if you work with younger learners – see **32**). Here's a simple example that works well with low level learners, and combines photos and text. Ask your learners to set three mobile phone alarms for a weekend day, e.g. at 10 am, 1 pm, and 5 pm. Set your own mobile alarms too, for a minute earlier. When each alarm rings, learners should each take a selfie, and share the photo in the class social network group with a caption describing where they are and what they are doing (e.g. *I'm at the supermarket doing the weekly shop; I'm playing in the park with my dog*; etc.). Do this yourself as well, posting your selfies a minute before the learners, so that your learners have a clear example of what's required. In class the following week, ask learners what they remember from the photos, as a quiz e.g. *What was Maria doing at 5 pm on Saturday?* This activity illustrates and practises the present versus past continuous, in a highly personalised and engaging way. (For this and more ideas on how to use mobile devices with learners, see the references below.)

Hockly, N. (2017). *ELTPedia Technology: 500 ideas for using technology in the English language classroom.* Pavilion Publishing and Media Ltd.

Hockly, N. and Dudeney, G. (2014). *Going Mobile.* Delta Publishing.

> Digital technologies have become increasingly embedded in teaching and learning, and this has led to a growing interest in whether – and how – teaching approaches need to adapt in response to this. Digital pedagogy attempts to answer the question, 'What does a pedagogically sound use of digital technologies in teaching and learning look like?'

At the simplest level, digital pedagogy can be understood as the use of digital technologies in the teaching (and learning) process. However, it's more than that. Rather than just focussing on how technologies can be integrated into existing practices, digital pedagogy invites questions as to how such technologies can be used to significantly improve and even transform these practices. Let's take an example to explore what this means.

A traditional approach to teaching a language point such as the second conditional might typically involve a teacher standing at the front of the class, writing example sentences on the board, and then highlighting the different grammatical components. In pairs, learners might then create more examples of second conditional sentences from prompts, to read out to the class. Let's now introduce some technology into this same lesson. The teacher follows the same procedures as above, but uses a PowerPoint presentation instead of the board to present and highlight the structure of the second conditional. Learners in pairs then produce their example sentences from prompts on one mobile device per pair, and share their sentences in a class WhatsApp group. Is this an example of good digital pedagogy? In short, not really. The use of digital technologies in this lesson does not really improve this lesson. The procedures, processes and outcomes are exactly the same in both versions of the lesson. If the digital technologies do not improve or transform the lesson, the teacher should ask him/herself whether they are worth using at all. Thus an understanding of digital pedagogy includes knowing when *not* to use digital technologies.

An example of a digital pedagogy that does potentially transform the teacher's role is the flipped classroom (see **14**). This approach enables the presentation and practice stages described above to be covered by learners before coming to class, for example, via an online video presentation and some online automated grammar activities. Time in the classroom can then be spent with learners taking part in communicative speaking activities that encourage the use of the target language (the second conditional). Here the flipped approach has changed the role of the teacher from expert to facilitator, and the use of technology by learners before the lesson has enabled that transition.

Further examples of effective digital pedagogy include learners recording a pair speaking activity on a mobile device to then analyse; or rehearsing, recording and sharing a personalised communicative speaking task via a class social network site. One final example: teachers can provide personalised and highly detailed feedback on a learner's written work by using **screencasting** software. Learners then use this individualised feedback to improve and resubmit their drafts. Although feedback could be written by the teacher by hand on the work, it would simply not be possible to provide the level of detail and guidance that screencasting with an audio commentary enables. Here we have a clear example of how technology can be used to improve teacher feedback.

Essentially, digital pedagogy requires that teachers have technical skills and are digitally literate (see **6**), but it also requires an understanding of the theories of learning that your teaching approaches often unconsciously reflect. Effective digital pedagogies harness technology not just for the transmission of information but for cooperative, collaborative and problem-solving approaches to learning. In these approaches, learners are given opportunities to work in pairs and groups, and to explore and learn by doing, supported by digital technologies. In other words, the use of digital technologies is driven by pedagogy, not the other way around.

Online learning design

Designing an online course can feel daunting. Apart from choosing a platform to deliver the course, there's the question of how to design online tasks that will support language learning. Let's look at a framework that can help.

Most teachers would agree that learning a language, whether in the physical classroom or online, should involve learners in a range of different interactions. Learners will need to interact with the course content, with the teacher, and with each other, at the very least. These interactions lead to the development of knowledge about the language through input, and they also enable the learner to practise the language in both spoken and written form, through output. So it stands to reason that if we develop an online language learning course, we should make sure that we design tasks that support both input and output.

In helping teachers and institutions design online language courses, I find it useful to not just refer to the need for input and output, but to also think about the kind of learning that each online task requires learners to engage in. This puts the emphasis on what *learners* need to do in a task, rather than on what the task itself looks like or contains. Diana Laurillard's Conversational Framework (see the UCL Knowledge Lab reference below) can support this more learner-centred approach to online task design. How?

Based on a range of learning theories, Laurillard's framework proposes six types of learning that we can use to guide our design of online and blended learning tasks/courses, for all age groups. The first type is *learning through acquisition*, where concepts are presented to learners, for example, by the teacher, the digital coursebook, and/or through online resources or multimedia. Tasks get learners to engage with these resources and (hopefully) acquire familiarity. Many online courses have no shortage of this kind of learning or task type. The second type is *learning through inquiry*, where tasks require learners to take a more active role. Perhaps learners need to research a topic online, or solve a problem, or ask the teacher questions about what has been presented in a live online class. The third type is *learning through practice*, where learners can put into practice what they've learned, for example, by writing an online quiz for classmates, or creating an online presentation. Related to this is *learning through discussion*, where learners can also apply what they've learned, but this time in a social context, for example by interacting with other learners and/or the teacher in a forum or in a live online class discussion. Similarly, *learning through collaboration* enables learners to practise what they've learned, but rather than simply discussing something, collaboration requires negotiation and agreement between learners; online tasks that support this type of learning will often require learners to *create* something together. Finally, there is *learning through production*; here learners will typically present their collaborative project/product to the teacher and classmates and get feedback, which in turn further enhances their learning. The learners' digital products or artefacts can form part of their ePortfolios (see **37**), and be assessed against previously shared criteria, if necessary.

As language teachers, we already use many of these types of learning, and tasks to support them, in our language classes. However, we are often in danger of prioritising *learning through acquisition* by focusing mainly on input, especially when it comes to designing online courses. With six types of learning, four of them supporting learner output, Laurillard's Conversational Framework provides us with a useful reminder that our online courses should include a range of task types, covering all of these learning types. Laurillard's free 'Learning Designer' online tool (see below) can help you design a sequence of online activities to include the various types of learning, and/or to analyse the pedagogic design of your online course.

UCL Knowledge Lab, UCL Institute of Education (2013–2021). *Learning Designer*. Available at: https://www.ucl.ac.uk/learning-designer/

C: Teaching language with learning technologies

When used appropriately, learning technologies can enhance our teaching of language (grammar, vocabulary and pronunciation), and of the four skills, in both the physical and virtual classroom. Learning technologies can also help us with feedback, assessment and evaluation.

> The internet provides us with a wealth of online texts.
> These texts often include hyperlinks, as well as multimedia
> that can support or enhance the written word. How can we
> use online texts to help develop our learners' reading skills?

Online texts include magazine and newspaper articles, **blog** posts, social media posts, **meme**s (see **25**) and more. Reading on a digital device has advantages for language learners. Why? Well, there are dictionary plug-ins and apps that work with computer browsers, mobile devices and e-readers. When a learner comes across a word in a digital text they don't understand, they can move their mouse over the unknown word (or touch the unknown word with their finger on a mobile device) and see an immediate translation. Having immediate access to translations of unknown words can help learners read faster and more easily, and so better understand a text; this increased comprehension can improve language learners' reading skills, according to some researchers (see the reference below).

What digital texts should we use in class? This depends on our learners' learning needs. For example, business English learners may need to read (and write) emails. English for Academic Puposes (EAP) learners may need to read (and write) academic articles online. Other learners may need or want to understand (and produce) social media updates, read hotel or restaurant reviews, or read product reviews (e.g. on a website like Amazon). Reading digital texts is not only a matter of understanding the English words on the digital page. The reader needs to be familiar with a range of other conventions, for example, the use of hashtags (#) in a social media update. Or the effects of **hyperlink**ing in an academic text, and how to reference online sources. How to understand (and use) these conventions may need to be explicitly taught. In addition, online texts are often **multimodal**. They can include non-verbal elements like images, audio and video. Understanding how these elements work can require visual and multimodal literacies, another area that we can explore in the classroom.

The length of the digital texts we choose needs to suit the technology that our learners use. Longer texts like online articles or blog posts are best read on desktop, laptop or tablet computers, because of the larger screen size. Shorter, more visual texts, like social media updates or memes, are well-suited to the smaller screens of mobile phones. Short social media texts, like Twitter tweets or Facebook or Instagram posts, are not traditional English language teaching texts, but they can give learners useful short, focused reading practice, particularly when learners themselves choose to follow social media celebrities who post in English (e.g. film, music or sporting stars). Ask your learners to share what they have learned about their chosen social media celebrities via social media, in class every couple of weeks. The more learners read English texts out of class, however short, the better!

Digital texts can also help learners develop other reading skills. Here's one simple activity that I like. Type out a text from a previous unit in the coursebook into a word-processed document. Then drag the paragraphs into the wrong order. In class, learners work in pairs on laptops to drag the paragraphs back into the correct order. A simple activity like this helps learners with text organisation, coherence and cohesion, and can be used with very low levels. In the next stage of the activity, learners work in pairs and choose different reading texts from previous units in the coursebook. One learner in each pair dictates the text while the other learner types it into a word processing program. The learners then put the paragraphs of their text into the wrong order, for another pair to rearrange into the correct order. This activity reviews language from the coursebook, and also works on reading skills. You can add an element of visual literacy by asking learners to add images to support their texts, and to explain their choices.

Li, J. (2009). 'The evolution of vocabulary learning strategies in a computer-mediated reading environment', *CALICO Journal*, 27, 1, 118–46.

19 Teaching listening

> Online resources that learners can use to practise listening include audio and video podcasts, narrated slideshows, and multimodal texts. I find that audio podcasts are a helpful source of listening materials for learners and can be used both in and outside the classroom.

Audio podcasts were one of the earliest **Web 2.0** technologies to interest educators. The fact that audio podcasts continue to be popular among language teachers and learners is testament to their usefulness. The term *podcast* is a combination of the words *iPod* (a portable MP3 player first produced by Apple in 2001), and *broadcast* (from the idea of a radio broadcast). A podcast is essentially a series of audio files that are produced regularly, and made available online. You can listen to a podcast online with an internet connection, or you can download it to your computer or mobile device and listen to it later without a connection. And therein lies their flexibility and longevity – you can listen to a podcast anytime, anywhere, on a mobile device. Personally, I try to develop my intermediate level French by listening to French radio podcasts on my mobile phone when doing household chores, and when I travel! Simply put, podcasts can provide learners with additional exposure to the target language outside the classroom, and this exposure, according to second language acquisition research, is definitely a good thing. For English language learners, there are many podcasts available online, from authentic radio programme podcasts such as those produced by the BBC or NPR, to podcasts specifically for learners produced by educational organisations like the British Council.

Over the years, I've seen podcasts used by teachers and learners in a variety of ways. Although teachers can limit themselves to simply recommending podcasts to their learners, there are more intentional ways in which they can be used to support language learning. For example, suggest a range of audio podcasts on topics that your learners may be interested in, and encourage them to listen to one or two podcasts over a period of time, e.g. once a week for a month. Listening to podcasts on a similar theme or area of interest to the learner means that important topic-specific vocabulary is likely to be repeated, increasing the likelihood of incidental learning. In class, ask the learners to briefly share one thing they learned from the podcast they listened to that week. It may be an interesting piece of information and/or a language point. After a month, get feedback from your learners on the experience of listening to podcasts and how useful they found it for language development. Encourage those learners who found it useful to continue listening to podcasts, and ask them to feed back regularly to the class on what they are learning. Reluctant listeners may be inspired to try more podcasts when they hear what their classmates are learning! The key to encouraging your learners to keep listening to podcasts is to integrate brief feedback on what they learn regularly into class time.

Learners can listen to podcasts, but learners (and teachers) can also relatively easily *produce* audio podcasts for classmates, the school, and the wider community. There are many advantages to having learners produce audio rather than video podcasts. Audio recording technology is easier to use than video technology, which may require editing. The production values in audio recording are less demanding for audio than for video: good audio is easily achieved by speaking directly into a mobile device's built-in microphone, whereas for video one needs to think about light, the framing of shots, appearance, sound quality at a distance, etc. Culturally, it may not be appropriate for learners to appear on video or learners may be reluctant to be filmed; audio, on the other hand, allows for a certain degree of anonymity. Learners generally feel less threatened when recording themselves in audio than in video, especially if they are speaking in a second or foreign language.

Live classes via video-conferencing have become increasingly popular in English language teaching; indeed, they are now often expected as part of a school's teaching offer. How can teachers make the most of this technology to deliver engaging – and secure – online classes?

Although free video-conferencing between teachers and learners has been possible since at least 2013, when Skype launched its free video messaging service, this technology was not that widely used in ELT. Understandably, teachers and learners preferred to practise speaking in the physical classroom. However, when the COVID-19 pandemic forced millions of learners and teachers online in early 2020, the potential of video-conferencing to support language learners in real time became apparent almost overnight. Video-conferencing tools like Skype and Zoom, among others, suddenly had millions of sessions per day, and webinars, online tutorials and training courses for teachers on how to use video-conferencing tools saw unprecedented uptake.

Providing online training and mentoring for teachers at this time, I had the opportunity to work with teachers in different contexts grappling with how to create and deliver engaging online language classes via video-conferencing. Here are a few considerations that can help you provide your English language learners with meaningful opportunities to practise speaking in video-conference lessons. They are divided into pedagogical considerations, technology and class management considerations, and considerations of wider issues around the use of video-conferencing, especially with learners under the age of 18.

Pedagogical considerations relate to the planning and delivery of your speaking activities or lessons. As with any free speaking activities in the physical classroom, including elements of personalisation (i.e. encouraging learners to talk about how the lesson content related to themselves), creating a reason for learners to want and need to listen to each other (i.e. an information gap), and ensuring a variety of speaking activities that are linked to the overall aims and content of the lessons, are important.

Using a video-conferencing tool also means paying attention to how the technology can support what we know about language learning. For the speaking skills, this means using video-conference breakout rooms regularly for pair and small group work, so that your learners get plenty of opportunities to produce the language, and to interact with each other. Your learners also need to have access to (and know how to use) their microphones, as well as appear on webcam. If cultural issues prevent learners from wanting to appear on camera in front of the whole class, negotiate the spaces in which they are willing to appear on camera, for example, in pairs or small groups in breakout rooms. Feeling confident with the technology is also important for the teacher. Take the time to learn about the various features of your chosen video-conferencing platform, and use them in the lesson where appropriate. For example, ask your learners to use icons to show agreement or disagreement; use the chat box to elicit short answers or to brainstorm, or to provide links to external tools that you use during the lesson, such as a Google Doc or Jamboard. Keeping learners engaged by asking them to use the various video-conferencing platform tools also shows you who is paying attention and who isn't! Manage your class effectively by providing one or two-minute mini-breaks in a class that lasts an hour or more, by asking your learners to go and fetch something to share with the group (e.g. three white objects; an item of food or clothing; an important personal object, etc.). For younger learners, including activities with movement is also important.

Finally, discuss the wider issues that can arise with video-conferencing with learners or parents/carers for younger learners. These include issues of privacy, recording (or not) of classes, and onboarding of parents to convince them of the value of live classes for speaking practice, especially if in-school classes are not an option in your context.

21 Teaching pronunciation

> To practise pronunciation, learners need to both recognise sounds and to produce sounds. Technology can help us in several ways with both stages of the process.

Regular practice with the sounds, rhythm and intonation of English can help your learners improve their pronunciation, and many coursebooks include elements of pronunciation. Typical pronunciation activities invite learners to identify and practise sounds and syllable stress in individual words, or word stress in sentences and longer stretches of discourse. Marking the intonation on sentences exemplifying functional language (e.g. question forms; polite requests, etc.), and then practising these sentences, is another typical pronunciation activity. In a physical classroom or live online lesson, you can model pronunciation features yourself, or you can play audio examples of these. To bring your learners' attention to certain sounds or prosodic features, you can mark these on the physical or virtual whiteboard during class, and then drill your learners in these elements of pronunciation. But the secret to effective language learning includes plenty of practice in the form of repetition and rehearsal, and learners are often not given much time to practise pronunciation in class, due to limited time and the pressures of completing a syllabus. This is where technology can help, by providing your learners with opportunities to work on their pronunciation individually, out of class time.

There are websites and apps that can provide learners with exposure to – and practice of – various elements of English pronunciation (sounds, word and sentence stress, and intonation). Mobile phone pronunciation or language learning apps can be particularly helpful for learners, who can easily take a few minutes in their day to listen to and practise their pronunciation, without needing to be in front of a desktop or laptop computer. Some English language coursebook publishers provide paid-for pronunciation apps (e.g. Macmillan's *Sounds* app), as do some large educational organisations (e.g. the British Council's *Sounds Right* app).

Free pronunciation apps can be found in mobile phone app stores; some are completely free, and some follow a freemium model. Some websites and pronunciation apps use speech recognition to score your learners' pronunciation on intelligibility. Notoriously unreliable in the past, speech recognition has improved markedly over the years and is now integrated into many programs and apps (e.g. WhatsApp), operating systems (e.g. Microsoft's Cortana and Apple's Siri), and home assistant devices (such as Google Home and Amazon's Alexa). Using programs and devices with speech recognition set to English enables learners to practise producing sentences and longer stretches of discourse, and to immediately see whether their utterances are intelligible.

However, using pronunciation websites, apps and speech recognition means that your learners' example words, sentences and stretches of discourse may not be very closely related to what they have worked on in class. One simple idea I especially like is to produce a weekly dictation audio podcast (see **19**) for learners, based on the content of the coursebook. The content of your dictation can be a short stretch of text from a reading in that week's coursebook unit, which your learners have already worked with, or it can be a new text that you write, which recycles the grammar and vocabulary from the unit in context. The aim is to provide your learners with a coherent stretch of discourse to enable them to practise prosodic features rather than individual words and sounds. How does it work? Learners first listen to your pre-prepared dictation and write it out, and check the accuracy of their writing – you can provide them with the written version of the dictation to check against. Learners then spend some time listening to your dictation line by line, repeating each line until they are able to produce the whole text relatively fluently, and they are happy with their pronunciation. It's important to remember that the aim of pronunciation is intelligibility, not for learners to lose their accents or to sound like a native speaker.

Learners need to be able to write different types of online texts, depending on their age, interests, and/or jobs. Younger learners, for example, are more likely to write short text messages and social media updates; adults are likely to need to write emails as part of their daily work.

With social media, messaging apps and email, our learners' daily lives probably involve a fair amount of communicative writing in their first language; this may consist of the very short texts favoured by social media and messaging apps. Online texts may also take the form of **blog** posts, contributions to online discussion forums, and online articles. Other online texts that learners may come across include **meme**s (see **25**), online presentations, and video subtitles. Our learners may read these latter online texts, but they are a lot less likely to be producing them in the real world. Let's look at how some of these online text types can develop learners' writing skills.

Popular social media platforms such as Facebook, Twitter and Instagram can expose learners to multimedia and texts in their own language, and also in English. I remember one elementary learner from Qatar proudly showing me on his mobile phone how he followed a well-known German DJ on Twitter, reading his tweets, which were written in English, and retweeting them to his own small number of Twitter followers, who were mainly his friends. Encouraging learners who already use popular social media platforms to follow celebrities who post social media updates in English – and even to respond to these updates in English – is one very effective way to get learners to produce their own micro texts in English. This kind of authentic writing can be highly motivating for learners. When a learner produces a tweet or status update for a real world audience in English, they will be keen to 'get it right', and will spend time checking and redrafting – both good writing practices.

Not all learners are social media users, so you may want to focus on other online text types for teaching writing. Blogging, which has been around since the early 2000s, can be used from primary-school aged learners to adults. Some researchers argue that writing blog posts for a real audience can motivate English language learners to write more accurately and to write longer texts. However, researchers also point out that learners do not automatically become more effective writers by creating blog posts, and teachers need to be realistic about what learners can achieve. Blogs do provide an opportunity for learners to develop the digital literacies that are needed to produce effective online texts, such as alternatives to using copyright images, correctly citing online sources, and avoiding plagiarism (see **36**). These are all part and parcel of online writing skills.

One online writing genre that many, if not most, learners use in their daily lives is instant messaging, usually via mobile phone apps like WhatsApp, Telegram or WeChat. Assuming that learners are of an appropriate age, a school-wide digital policy is in place (see **32**), and it is culturally appropriate to do so, you could set up an instant messaging group for a class, in which your learners can practise short-form writing in English. What's particularly interesting about written instant messages is that they reflect many of the characteristics of spoken language. For example, intonation and tone can be conveyed via emoticons; words written in capitals can mimic surprise or shouting. In fact, researchers have found that taking part in text chat activities can prepare learners for speaking activities by decreasing anxiety, especially at lower levels of proficiency (see the reference below). Writing instant messages in English can be a stepping stone to speaking, so if appropriate, it may be worth encouraging your learners to use it.

Satar, H. M. and Ozdener, N. (2008). 'The effects of synchronous CMC on speaking proficiency and anxiety: Text versus voice chat', *Modern Language Journal*, 92, 4, 595–613.

> Mobile devices can be especially effective at providing learners with opportunities to learn and practise new vocabulary. Let's look at how.

There are two main approaches to teaching vocabulary via mobile devices. The most common approach is a *content*-based approach, which delivers lexical items to learners' mobile phones, for example via vocabulary apps, or via regular quizzes, SMS texts, or group messaging texts from the teacher. The second is a *task*-based approach. This draws on affordances (or features) of mobile phones to provide learners with learning experiences via tasks that require understanding and using vocabulary. For example, in one study (Wong, L-H. and Looi, C-K., 2010), small groups of learners superimposed objects around the school to create 'sculptures' to illustrate various prepositions of place. They then took photos of their sculptures, and shared them with the class, describing their sculptures using prepositions of place. However, as this example shows, it can be challenging to design tasks that reflect an effective balance of time and effort versus learning opportunities. In other words, the amount of time and effort involved in carrying out a task like this, when compared with the amount of vocabulary practice it generated, is arguably not the best use of class time. So, how can teachers provide opportunities for the creative learning of new vocabulary, both in and outside the physical or online classroom, via mobile devices? One answer is: with flashcard apps.

Before we look in more detail at flashcard apps, it's worth keeping in mind the three essential stages that researchers propose are needed for effective vocabulary learning: 1) the learner notices the new word; 2) the learner encounters the word several times and is thus able to retrieve it; and 3) the learner is able to use the new word creatively in new contexts. Vocabulary apps often present learners with new words, and then practise these words through spaced repetition, covering the first two stages; the downside is that the vocabulary presented by some popular vocabulary apps can be decontextualized and of questionable usefulness. Nevertheless, content-based vocabulary apps or approaches can help learners with the important first stages of vocabulary learning – exposure, recognition and retrieval.

Flashcards have been a popular way to teach vocabulary for a very long time. Digital flashcards can include multimedia, such as audio, to help learners with the pronunciation of lexical items. Flashcards can also include definitions, translations, images or video. Many popular vocabulary apps include ready-made flashcard sets, which teachers can use to present new lexis, and learners can use to practise this new lexis out of class. However, some popular flashcard apps (e.g. Memrise, Quizlet and Anki) enable teachers and learners to produce their own flashcard sets; this provides an opportunity for a more creative use of lexis already learned, and enables teachers and learners to work with new vocabulary in ways that can combine a content-based *and* a task-based approach. In a content-based approach, learners use flashcards sets provided by the app itself, or created by the teacher. However, in a task-based approach, learners produce their *own* flashcard sets for review, which requires both understanding and applying new lexis, for example, by providing new example sentences and/or images on the flip side of each flashcard, as well as recording the pronunciation. Because the cards are in digital format, they can easily be shared with classmates, who can also play with them, leading to further reinforcement and practice of vocabulary. Imagine a class of 20 learners working in pairs, with each pair producing a flashcard set of ten items to review a different lexical area. In total there will be 100 flashcards (i.e. individual vocabulary items) produced, covering ten different vocabulary areas, and which learners can then review out of class time, multiple times. This arguably reflects a good balance between time invested and learning opportunities provided.

Wong, L-H. and Looi, C-K. (2010). 'Vocabulary learning by mobile-assisted authentic content creation and social meaning making: Two case studies', *Computer-Assisted Learning*, 26, 5, 421–33.

> Teaching grammar involves not just helping our learners
> understand a grammatical structure, but also giving them
> plenty of opportunities to use the language in meaningful
> ways. Technology can support both of these stages.

When teachers ask me, 'How can I teach grammar with technology?',
they often mean, 'How can I teach the first conditional (or modal verbs,
or the past continuous) with technology?' The other thing teachers often
mean by this question is, 'How can I *present* the first conditional (or
modal verbs, or the past continuous) to my learners with technology?'
Teaching grammar is often seen as a presentation activity – something
that teachers tell learners about, often with the use of a whiteboard
and example sentences, whether in a physical classroom or online in a
virtual classroom.

Of course, our learners need to know *about* grammar, but they also
need to be able to *use* the grammar to communicate with others. To
help our learners acquire knowledge about a target grammar point,
technology can provide several alternatives to the live, in-class, teacher-
led presentation. For example, we can video record ourselves in advance
explaining a grammar point, possibly as if we were in the classroom,
that is, to camera with a portable whiteboard. Or we could prepare
some PowerPoint or Google slides with our chosen grammar point,
and record an audio voiceover with the slideshow. In both cases, our
learners can watch the grammar presentation before coming to class –
this is an example of the flipped classroom approach (see **14**). We also
need to provide our learners with examples of our chosen grammar
point in context, and within longer stretches of discourse. For this, we
can provide our learners with an online text and/or an online video that
includes examples of our target language in context. Indeed, we could
start the teaching process here, to see how much learners already know
about the chosen grammar point – it may not be necessary to present
the language to them at all.

Whether we include a grammar presentation stage or not, we definitely need to give learners an opportunity to practise the target language. Online grammar games and apps can provide controlled practice for learners that can easily be done in their own time, or in pairs in class. We also need to provide learners with the opportunity to use a chosen grammar point more creatively, and in wider spoken and written contexts. Pair and group work speaking activities with prompts or discussion points (in the physical classroom, or in breakout rooms in live online classes) can easily provide this practice, but technology can enable you to design some additional creative activities. One simple awareness-raising activity uses two-way translations (see **41**).

Another creative idea is to run a Grammar Safari with your learners.

- For a higher level group, prepare a worksheet with tasks such as:

    1. Find an example of one sentence with two modal verbs.
    2. Find an example of a third conditional sentence beginning with 'Had …'.
    3. Find an example of a reported command.
    4. Find an example of a separated phrasal verb.
    5. Find an example of the past passive tense.

    And so on, up to about ten examples. For a lower level group, include less complex grammatical forms.

- Then direct the learners to a website that consists entirely of texts: it could be an online newspaper, or a collection of literary texts such as The Gutenberg Project (http://www.gutenberg.org/ebooks/).
- In pairs or small groups, students race to find examples of all the grammar points. You may first need to show your learners how to search a website page (on a PC, you can pull up a key word search bar by holding down the ctrl + F keys).
- Once a few groups have finished, stop the activity, and ask each group to share their examples. Award points for each correct example. You could ask for another example using the same structure for bonus points, to add a level of additional challenge.
- Ask each group to add up their points to see who wins!

As a lingua franca, English is used in many intercultural and cross-cultural settings, so in our digitally networked world, cultural competence is essential. Let's look at how we can help our learners develop their intercultural literacy through a particularly popular internet phenomenon: memes.

Memes are **digital artefacts** with images, texts, audio and/or video that spread quickly via the internet, with users often making slight variations to the meme before sharing. Memes can be very amusing, and they often poke fun at current trends, events or beliefs. We all love a good meme, and because of this, they can be used by teachers to develop learners' cultural awareness alongside language and digital skills, while promoting creativity – and just plain fun! Memes exist in global internet culture, often in English, but they also exist in our learners' local languages. A global digital trend reflected in an English-language meme can be taken up and re-interpreted in a local language. As such, memes are both cross-cultural and local, and they provide teachers with a unique opportunity to work with learners on their English language, intercultural literacy *and* digital skills.

One of the most enduring English language memes is 'Keep Calm and Carry On', a poster that displays these words in white caps on a red background, topped by a crown. The poster was originally printed by the British Government as propaganda during the Second World War; it was rediscovered in the year 2000, and shared on the internet in 2007. A spoof version of this poster soon appeared, with a blue background, an upside down crown, and the words 'Now Panic and Freak Out' in the same font. The website Keep Calm-o-matic, which enables users to easily make their own versions of the meme, launched in 2009, and tens of thousands of versions of the meme have been created since. Some memes endure; others are short-lived, responding to specific events in politics or in popular culture. Some memes become popular internationally (e.g. the Dancing Coffin meme); others remain closely tied to local context. (To see these memes, search for them on the *Know your meme* website: https://knowyourmeme.com)

How can you work with memes with your learners? In my training workshops, I often recommend the following approach. An essential part of cultural competence is an ability to observe and think critically about one's own culture, so analysing memes that your learners know in their own language/country is a good first step. You could share one of your favourite local memes with your class, and ask each learner to choose another favourite meme to share. This is a good opportunity to discuss with your learners what cultural messages or assumptions underlie each meme, what makes them work, and why they think their chosen memes are successful. You can then move on to examining memes in English. Your learners may already be familiar with some English language memes, and in this case, pairs of learners could choose one to work with. But if your learners don't know any memes in English, you can assign one to each pair. The first step is for each pair of learners to research their chosen meme online (the Know your meme website and Wikipedia are good sources), to find at least two or three variations of the original meme, and to then present what they have learned about the meme to the class. Again, for each meme, discuss with the class what cultural messages or assumptions underlie each meme, and what they think of it.

By this stage, learners have had the opportunity to view and analyse a range of memes and should be ready to create their own memes. Learners can create a meme online through a free meme generator website or app (search for "meme generator"), or on paper. Working in the same pairs, encourage your learners to create a version of the meme they presented earlier to the class, or to choose any meme they like to create their own variation. Finally, your learners should share their memes with their classmates.

26 Correction and feedback online

Learners expect to be corrected, and to receive feedback on their work. Providing this for your learners is not just about meeting their expectations; receiving feedback – and acting on it – is an essential part of the learning process. But if we teach fully online, how can we best correct and provide feedback?

Many of the real time correction and feedback practices that teachers use in the physical classroom can fairly easily be done in a live online class. For example, imagine that your learners carry out a speaking activity in pairs or small groups in the physical classroom, while you walk around and monitor, noting any common or important errors on a piece of paper rather than interrupting the learners while they are talking. Once the activity has finished, you hold a brief correction slot, writing the errors you noted down on the board, and inviting the class to correct each error together. A correction slot can be carried out in a live online class too. Your learners can carry out the speaking activity in breakout rooms while you monitor, moving from virtual room to virtual room and noting down the common errors. You can note down these errors in a word processing document on your computer, or in Google docs or on a slide, so that you can easily share the errors with the learners after the speaking activity, once they are back in the main video-conferencing room. In this case, we use the technology to mimic how we deliver personalised correction/feedback in the physical classroom.

Technology can also provide us with ways to provide automated and more generic feedback. For example, you can create an online grammar or vocabulary quiz for your learners, in which they need to choose or type the correct answers. Some online quiz tools will allow you to add tips or hints to help learners, and if they get an answer wrong, the quiz can display feedback that gives them further help or information, and encourages them to try again to improve their score. By creating your own quizzes for your learners, you can write automated feedback to address the mistakes you know they are likely to make. For example, if you create a quiz about personality adjectives for learners who are Spanish speakers, you know that they may confuse the adjectives *sensible* and *sensitive*, because *sensible* in Spanish is a false friend (it means *sensitive*). For a quiz question that asks learners to choose the correct personality adjective, you can write a hint like, 'Remember that *sensible* in English has a different meaning to *sensible* in Spanish!'

If you're teaching online, you may also need to provide feedback on your learners' writing in online discussion forums. Providing feedback on this kind of asynchronous written interaction is not the same as providing feedback on an individual learner's written assignment or essay. Communication and interaction are key elements of successful online forum discussions; with this in mind, you should give your learners feedback not just on their use of language, but also on whether they are interacting effectively or not. If effective interaction/communication is part of your online assessment criteria (see **28**), it is only fair to give your learners ongoing feedback about how successfully (or not) they are communicating, with advice on how to improve this. Indeed, effective feedback provides learners with the information they need to do things more successfully next time – essentially *feedback* becomes *feedforward*, with learners able to apply lessons learned to what they do next.

Finally, if your learners submit their written work in a word-processed document, you can add comments to provide feedback or suggestions, or you can use 'track changes' to reformulate or correct their writing. You can also use screen capture software (e.g. Snagit or Camtasia) to provide spoken feedback on a piece of written work; in this case you essentially video record yourself talking through a learner's written work while highlighting areas for improvement and providing suggestions and corrections.

27 Automated writing evaluation

Programs that can automatically correct and grade learners' written work have been around for well over a decade. How useful are they to English language teachers and learners?

Automated writing evaluation (AWE) software, also known as automated essay scoring (AES) software, compares a learner's essay or composition with a large corpus of model writing. An AWE program uses computational thinking to analyse areas in the text (e.g. word count, range of vocabulary, spelling, organisation, coherence), and assigns it an overall score. An AWE program can provide suggested corrections for vocabulary and grammar, and also gives standardised feedback comments on the learner's overall writing style and/or level. Although this kind of software has the potential to reduce the marking of written work that often makes up a considerable amount of a teacher's workload, it is only as good as the corpus/database that is used as a reference.

Of course, like all educational technology software, there are pros and cons to AWE. On the plus side, the use of AWE can encourage learners to review their writing in the light of the automated feedback they receive, it increases learners' motivation for writing, and learners often report having positive attitudes to AWE. For EFL learners, the automated feedback provided by AWE on language use can also improve the accuracy of their writing. On the minus side, research shows that learners are sometimes critical of the accuracy of AWE feedback and scoring (see the reference below). In addition, although learners see the value of receiving AWE feedback on their writing, teachers don't often schedule class time for learners to *review* their writing in the light of this feedback. Reviewing and redrafting are good writing practices that can improve learners' written work, so teachers miss an important opportunity to support their learners' writing by missing out this step.

The potential of AWE for English teachers lies in its use in formative assessment, rather than summative assessment. The ability of AWE to identify issues with vocabulary range and grammatical accuracy, and to provide feedback on this, enables language learners to redraft and improve their written texts, especially at lower levels.

If you'd like to try using AWE to support your learners writing, I'd suggest a step-by-step approach. First, show your learners a free online AWE program like *Write&Improve* or *The Writing Mentor* (for EAP), and explore how the program works with your learners in class. For homework, ask your learners to each create a short text, to use the AWE program, and to revise their texts based on the feedback provided by the program. Ask your learners to then submit their revised texts with the AWE feedback, so that you can see how they have incorporated that feedback. Provide your own feedback on how effectively they have revised their texts. Finally, discuss with your learners how useful they think the program is as a developmental tool for their writing. Ask them to use it over a period of time (e.g. a month or two), periodically reviewing the AWE feedback and their drafts with them, and discussing how helpful (or not) they are finding it. For AWE to be effective, learners need to see that the program actually helps improve their writing, and teachers need to provide support for their learners in how to use it effectively. It's useful to remember that AWE is most effective with formulaic and less creative writing though. So if you're getting your learners to write poetry, it's best to avoid using AWE to assess their efforts!

Warschauer, M. and Grimes, D. (2008). 'Automated writing assessment in the classroom', *Pedagogies*, 3, 1, 52–67.

28 Digital evaluation and assessment

Assessing learners' digital or online work brings with it a unique set of considerations. Of course, you will want to assess your learners' use of language, but you will also want to assess the digital component of their work.

Digital assessment is a large field. The term can refer to computer-based testing, which may utilise technologies such as automated writing evaluation (see **27**) in high-stakes exams. On a smaller scale, individual teachers or schools may create their own computer-based tests, including automated quizzes or tests to assess learners' knowledge of language; these sorts of self-grading tests are often complemented with writing and speaking tests assessed by teachers, to include the productive skills. Technologies can also be used in alternative forms of assessment such as ePortfolios (see **37**), or collaborative digital projects.

How do we assess our learners' digital or online work? Well, this depends on what you are assessing. For example, do you want to assess your learners' written contributions to asynchronous forum discussions in a **VLE** (**virtual learning environment**), or do you want to assess their spoken contributions to a live video-conference class? Do you want to assess their **blog** posts, or PowerPoint presentations, or the audio or video recordings they have made as a response to a task? Each of these examples requires your learners to produce written and/or spoken English, but they use very different digital modes and mediums, which also need to be taken into account for assessment. This suggests that we need to tailor our assessment for each of these examples. To ensure that learners know what we are assessing and why, it can be helpful to use rubrics that include language *and* digital criteria, which should be shared with learners in advance.

For example, assessing a learner's written contributions to online discussion forums can involve not just their use of English, but also how effectively they interact or respond to previous forum posts by classmates. After all, a forum discussion shouldn't just be a series of disconnected written statements, but should form part of a *discussion*, so does the learner acknowledge other learners' contributions, and develop the discussion effectively by bringing new ideas? Are their responses relevant? Does the learner respond in a timely manner to the task, and more than once? Apart from assessing language in a forum discussion, these criteria of interactivity, quality, relevance, promptness, and frequency should also be included in your assessment rubric.

In the case of assessing a learner's written contributions to a class blog, we may want to include slightly different criteria in a rubric, apart from language use. Learners are likely to include **hyperlinks** and images in their blog posts, and these should form part of the assessment. For example, is the hyperlinking judicious and effective, or do too many hyperlinks make the blog posts difficult to read, or are they linked to unreliable sources? As we saw in **6**, effective hyperlinking is an important digital literacy, so you should not only teach this to your learners if you want them to blog effectively, but also include it in assessment. The effective use of images by respecting copyright, and including one's online sources, are other criteria that can be included in a rubric for the assessment of blog posts.

And what of assessing a learner's speaking in a live online video-conference class? In this particular case, we can focus almost exclusively on language. But I always suggest to teachers that they don't assess everything, because this can have an inhibiting effect on learners wanting to contribute. Rather, tell learners exactly what spoken interactions will be assessed and when, and allow them a little preparation time for the assessed speaking task, e.g. in breakout rooms. In this particular case, the technology (a breakout room) can be used to support and prepare your learners for assessment.

D: Managing learning technologies

Using learning technologies effectively includes understanding – and knowing how to deal with – some of the wider issues that surround their use. Some issues are especially relevant to using technologies with younger learners, while some affect adults as well.

> **Digital tools can help teachers promote positive learner practices in their physical or online classes, especially among their younger learners.**

Let's take a look at why and how you might want to use digital classroom management tools, especially if you teach young learners or teens.

When I was at primary school, I was what they call a 'late developer'. At the age of six I remember struggling to understand the concept of clocks and time. One particularly difficult classroom activity (to me) had me sitting with a worksheet alone, trying and failing to draw the time on a seemingly endless row of blank clock faces, while my classmates had already finished and gone outside to play. My teacher had a reward system for completing work: a chart on the wall with a tick next to each learner's name when they finished. There was a glaring blank next to my name, and how I longed for that tick! The teacher helped me complete the worksheet. I got my tick. In the next class, when more dreaded blank clock faces were handed out, my teacher pointed out how well we were *all* doing. Even if I got my tick on the chart a little later than everyone else, I'd still get that tick.

Many classroom management apps for young learners capitalise on this sort of extrinsic motivation, by rewarding achievement and good behaviour. These apps go well beyond the kind of paper-based achievement chart that was popular in my primary school days. One of the most popular classroom management apps for primary aged learners at the time of writing is Class Dojo (https://www.classdojo.com/), which enables teachers to assign points or badges to their learners and/or to the whole class for achievements or positive behaviours in a range of areas (e.g. good team work, accurate spelling, completing homework on time, arriving on time for class, not giving up easily, paying attention – and many more). It also enables teachers to subtract points for negative behaviours (e.g. arriving late, not doing homework, misbehaviour, etc.), although teachers do not necessarily have to use the negative points system. Teachers can set up their own reward systems for their learners, assigning (or subtracting) points for behaviours that they identify as important. The app also enables teachers to communicate directly with parents via a messaging system, and to share class work, including photos and images. Some primary school teachers have told me that they find referring to a child's progress in the app during parent-teacher meetings extremely useful.

If keeping classroom noise to an acceptable level is important for you, there are several free web-based apps that help teachers monitor the noise in a classroom, such as Calm Counter (https://calmcounter. ictgames.com/) or Bouncy Balls (https://bouncyballs.org/). These kinds of apps tend to come and go, but a search on your mobile phone app store for 'noise monitor' will give you several more apps to try out.

Classroom management apps can help teachers of younger learners track and reward good behaviours. For teachers of adults, **Virtual Learning Environments** (**VLE**s) can fulfil a similar function. Most VLEs include learner tracking (see **39**), which gathers detailed information about a learner's attendance, engagement with learning materials, and participation (e.g. in discussion forums). This can help the teacher identify those learners who show strong performances in any of these areas, and the teacher may reward this by praising good work publicly to the class, or even awarding badges or points if appropriate.

Whatever classroom management tools you decide to try, your learners need to understand how they work and what each tool will be used for. Make sure you show and discuss the tools with your learners, so that they are clear on expected behaviours – and on the all-important rewards.

Teachers sometimes worry about learners getting distracted if they use their own mobile devices in the classroom. To combat this, effective task design and device management are key.

There are strategies that teachers can use to minimise distraction, and to keep learners on task, even when they use their own devices in class. One of the most important strategies is to design effective and engaging mobile-based tasks. If your learners are taking part in a well-structured and meaningful task that requires the use of a mobile device, and that has a clear timeframe and outcome, they are less likely to get distracted. Effective mobile-based tasks should encourage interaction between learners, providing situations where they need to use English to communicate. To ensure that you have interaction and communication while your learners are using their mobile devices, you can encourage pair and group work. Below is an example to show how this can work in practice.

One activity I particularly like is 'Five-minute photo race', which takes advantage of learners using their own personal devices. Put the learners in pairs, then give them a list of seven to ten photos that they each need to find on their phones, and share with their partner. Your list of photos to find might include: a party or celebration; a close friend; a family member; a photo in the countryside; a photo of themselves doing a sport; a selfie they particularly like; a pet; etc. For each photo, learners need to share with their partner who is in the photo, and where and when it was taken. Give learners five minutes to complete the activity, and time it! After five minutes, stop the activity and ask the learners to put their phone face-down on their desks, where you can see them. It's quite difficult to get learners' attention back from an activity like this, so you need to ensure that this device management step is included. Then nominate pairs to share one thing they learned about their partner from the activity. For homework, you can ask learners to choose one of the photos they shared and to write a short paragraph about the photo. Learners can then share their chosen photo in a class social networking group, or **blog**.

This simple speaking activity illustrates several strategies that help with managing mobile devices in the classroom. The activity is engaging because it's personalised – learners of all ages love to share information (and photos!) about themselves. It has an explicit and clear outcome. It has a time limit, so learners don't really have a chance to do something else like check social media. Ideally, the time limit should be slightly shorter than the time needed to fully complete the task, which also creates a sense of urgency. Finally, having learners put their devices face-down on the desk where you can clearly see them (or to put them away in their bags) removes the distraction and enables you to move on to the next stage of the task. Creating these clear stages in classroom management helps learners know when it's time to look at their devices, and when it's time to put them away. The task goes beyond the classroom as well, with learners sharing additional information about a chosen photo in written form, for homework. Mobile devices can be very effectively used to bridge in-class and out-of-class work in this way.

Teachers who use mobile devices in the classroom with younger learners and teenagers may have additional concerns about how to manage the devices effectively. We look at strategies that are particularly important when working with young learners and mobile devices in **31** and **32**.

> An acceptable use policy (AUP) can help learners use
> mobile devices at school appropriately and safely.

There are many reasons why teachers may want their learners to
use mobile devices in the classroom in support of learning (see 30,
32). But teachers of young learners and teenagers may have concerns
about misuse of devices, such as the devices being used for sharing
inappropriate content, for **cyberbullying** or **sexting,** or for audio- or
video-recording the teacher and classmates without permission.
Children and adolescents are learning to navigate their identities and
to form friendships in the digital world as much as in the physical
world, but they may be less aware of what constitutes appropriate
and inappropriate practices in the digital sphere, unless these are
specifically taught. Digital literacies such as e-safety and online identity
management are often integrated into the wider curriculum these days
precisely to help learners develop online practices that are acceptable
and desirable, and to understand which are not.

Integrating digital literacies into the curriculum (including in the English
language classroom – see 6) is therefore the first step in encouraging
the appropriate use of mobile devices in school. The second step is to
have a robust acceptable use policy (AUP) in place, as part of a wider
school digital policy (see 32). In essence, an AUP clearly sets out the
consequences of misusing mobile devices at school. For example, video-
recording a class or the teacher without permission might result in a
learner's mobile device being confiscated by the school for 24 hours.
More serious issues, such as cyberbullying, require that the school
director and parents get involved at the very least; in some cases,
cyberbullying may even involve the police.

Given that AUPs are most often used with primary and secondary-
aged learners, parents need to be informed of the content of a school
AUP from the beginning. Ideally, an AUP is developed *before* teachers

and learners start using mobile devices in the classroom, and all the stakeholders, including parents, are aware of and agree with the AUP contents. However, it's never too late to draw up an AUP. It's also important that parents agree with the terms in an AUP, as confiscating a child's mobile phone needs parental permission. Parents can be informed about AUPs by email, and parent/teacher meetings can be held at the beginning of a new term, so that parents can discuss any concerns they may have around the use of mobile devices in school. In cases of misuse, parents should be informed.

AUPs do not necessarily need to be imposed by the director or school as a top-down decision. The most effective AUPs are negotiated, with learners encouraged to suggest their own rules for what they consider appropriate – and inappropriate – use. No child wants to be cyberbullied, or to have their classmates using mobile phones in ways that can harm them; children will typically be in favour of fair play when it comes to the use of mobiles in the classroom and within the school grounds. A negotiated AUP can be created as a schoolwide project, with all classes being involved in contributing to an acceptable use charter. The final version of the charter is voted on, and then signed by teachers, children *and* parents. Schools can also update parents on effective uses of mobile devices, by sharing examples of the mobile-based work that learners produce. It's worth remembering that rewarding the appropriate use of mobile devices is as important as dissuading inappropriate behaviour.

A digital policy (or e-policy) describes how digital devices and software can or should be used in an educational institution. As more technologies are used by teachers and learners, so schools need robust digital policies for a range of possible use scenarios, as well as to comply with legislation.

Many educational institutions have had some sort of digital policy in place for years. When I started teaching at a language school in Spain in the late 1980s, parents were asked to sign a consent form for learners under 18 at the beginning of each school year. This form allowed parents to give (or refuse) permission for the school to take photos of their children on school excursions or occasionally in class, and then use those photos in a school magazine or brochure. These were the days before schools had websites, but when those came along, consent forms were typically extended to cover the use of images in the digital sphere.

Safeguarding against possible misuse of technologies, through acceptable use policies (see **31**), is just one aspect of a more comprehensive digital policy. Let's not forget that schools have a responsibility towards their learners, whatever their age, and need to respect learners' privacy and protect their data. For example, if your school uses a **VLE** and/or a video-conferencing platform for online teaching, exactly what happens to learner data needs to be clear. For example, who has the right to view and track learners' use of the VLE? Who stores this data, where is it stored, and for how long? And if you record your live video-conferencing classes with your learners, what happens to these recordings? Who can view them, and for what purposes? Issues of privacy are an important area to include in your institution's overall digital policy, and the policy needs to comply with legislation in your state, province or country.

For example, at the time of writing, the Personal Information Protection Act (PIPA) in the province of British Columbia in Canada means that educational institutions are not allowed to use external web tools or platforms that have servers located in the USA. This means that teachers can't legally use popular tools like Padlet or Google Docs, or VLEs with US-based servers, with their learners. Similarly, the introduction of GDPR (General Data Protection Regulation) in the European Union in 2018 has had important consequences for data privacy, and how learners' personal information is collected and processed. In previous times, a teacher might have passed a piece of paper around class to collect learners' emails, at the beginning of a new school year. This is no longer legal, as it does not provide for safe electronic storage of the data, and nor does it give learners the opportunity to voluntarily opt in, or to have their data deleted at a future date. The onus is on institutions and teachers, not learners, to comply with privacy and data legislation. If you would like to check your school's compliance with privacy legislation, looking at a range of institutions' websites can give you a good idea of how others are complying with these often complex laws. Many university and school websites have an explanation of how they comply with legislation like GDPR, for example. Apart from complying with privacy legislation, schools sometimes include an educational agenda in their digital policies. For example, they include objectives such as developing learners' (and teachers') digital literacies, or ensuring that their curricula integrate a pedagogically sound use of technology.

As new learning technologies find their way into the language classroom, and as privacy laws change, a school's digital policy can become outdated. Reviewing the policy regularly is essential. Schools that don't yet have a digital policy should develop one. There are digital policies for primary, secondary and tertiary institutions freely available online, so there is no need to start from scratch. A web search will provide plenty of examples.

Keeping learners safe online (e-safety) is often associated with teaching minors. But there are many aspects of digital safety that affect adults as well.

Like the physical world, the online world can harbour dangers that we want to protect ourselves and our children from. This is best done through education. Much as we teach children not to touch a hot stove in order to avoid a burn, so we should be teaching them to not click blindly on a **hyperlink** in order to avoid inadvertently downloading **malware**. Knowing how to stay safe online is an essential part of being digitally literate, and many schools start teaching safe online practices from primary school. Teaching children about e-safety will often include discussing issues such as **cyberbullying**, managing personal information online, responsible social media practices, and how to deal with viruses and malware. A comprehensive e-safety syllabus should include helping children understand safe practices in online social spaces, but also how to deal with technology-based issues such as malware.

Despite the emphasis on e-safety for youngsters, there is also a case to be made for educating adults in safe online practices. Not all adults received robust e-safety education at school, and the adult online world is as prone to anti-social behaviours as that inhabited by younger learners. One area of particular relevance to adults is that of identity theft and online fraud, for example. And as regular email users, adults are prime targets for **phishing** emails and other online scams. However, although online dangers exist, we need to be careful about over-reacting. Only a small percentage of online users ever suffer these abuses; being well-informed and proactive is the key. This means teaching our learners to identify aberrant online behaviour, and having strategies to deal with issues if they should ever arise.

Given the importance of e-safety for younger learners, there are many websites dedicated to this topic, with a wealth of educational resources for learners, parents and teachers. Two websites that I particularly recommend are the NSPCC (National Society for the Prevention of Cruelty to Children), which has a section dedicated to online safety: https://www.nspcc.org.uk/keeping-children-safe/online-safety/, and Childnet https://www.childnet.com/. Both of these sites have advice, tips, checklists, and video resources for educators.

Finally, here are some e-safety activities you can do with learners from different age groups:

1. e-Safety poster (suitable for primary-aged learners): Learners first brainstorm safe practices online, and then create paper-based or online posters in small groups. The Childnet site has examples of online posters for a range of ages.
2. Discuss cyberbullying (suitable for teenagers): Have a short discussion about cyberbullying, e.g. what it is, and whether your learners have heard of (or experienced) any examples of it. Show them this short award-winning film about cyberbullying from Childnet: http://goo.gl/fCkNn1 and discuss it afterwards.
3. Social media settings (suitable for teenagers and adults): Ask learners what social media sites they use, and what privacy settings they have in place. Many learners simply retain default privacy settings. Put learners into small groups to research the settings of a social media site they use, and to make changes to their own social media privacy settings based on what they learn. Share and discuss what changes learners made and why.
4. Phishing (suitable for adults): Assign pairs of learners the terms *phishing, spear phishing* or *whaling* to research online in class, with a time limit. Regroup the learners to share what they have learned about each term. The terms refer to various forms of message-based internet fraud that cause an unsuspecting individual to click on an unsafe link; these attacks are often initiated via email. In their groups, learners brainstorm ways to spot and avoid these attacks. Finally, share and discuss these strategies with the whole class.

> The issue of copyright and the internet is a notoriously grey area. What online materials can – and can't – be legally reused by teachers and learners can be confusing. There are some guidelines, however, that can help teachers understand this complex area.

Having worked in technology training for over two decades, I find that many teachers believe that if an image, audio, video, article or any other piece of material is freely available online, it's OK to use it with learners. This is simply not true. For example, imagine that you want to add images of animals to a word-processed worksheet of vocabulary that you are preparing for a group of your learners. Typically, you might search online in Google Images or similar, find the images you like, and then download them to add to your worksheet. Some images might have a watermark indicating that they are copyrighted, so you probably won't download those, unless you decide to pay for them. But other images don't seem to have any copyright marking, not even the small © symbol that typically denotes copyright. So it's acceptable to download those images, right? Wrong. The default mode for online content created by others is that it is copyrighted, unless otherwise indicated. So even when images (or any **digital artefacts**) have no overt copyright marks, they are in fact copyrighted, and by downloading them, you are technically breaking the law.

Does this mean that it's not possible to use anything at all that you find online? Not at all. It simply means you need to be aware of a number of key concepts in the area of digital copyright and to respect them. The first concept is *Creative Commons*. Online content (e.g. text, images, and multimedia) that is freely available for others to use will have a Creative Commons license applied. We explore Creative Commons in **35** in more depth, but suffice it to say at this point that a Creative Commons license will usually enable you to reuse content as long as you respect the conditions of the license.

A second important concept is that of *fair use*, also referred to in some countries as *fair dealing*. Fair use enables educators to use a small percentage of copyrighted work without getting formal permission from the creator. However, fair use is an *exception* to copyright, and it is limited to a number of very specific uses: news reporting and commentary, criticism and parody, research, and teaching/education. Let's take another example to try and clarify the concept of fair use. Imagine that you would like to share a chapter from a copyrighted book with a group of university students in an English for Academic Purposes (EAP) class. If this chapter is a small percentage of the total book (around five to ten percent is generally agreed to be the limit), then it is acceptable to share this content with your learners – in principle. However, one of the limits to fair use is that the content cannot be used for commercial purposes. So, if you teach in a private language school or fee-paying university, it could be argued that sharing the chapter falls under commercial use because your learners are paying for classes. Fair use is very unclear on this point. In order to be certain that you don't break the law, if the chapter is already available online, it would be best to share the **hyperlink** with your learners, so that they read the chapter at source. Fair use can be applied to online text, audio and video, where you can conceivably use five to ten percent of the material. Images are a different matter though, as it impossible to share just a small percentage of an image. We explore how to legally use online images in **35**.

Creative Commons is a movement that aims to provide an alternative to often strict online copyright laws. Let's see how creators can apply different kinds of Creative Commons licences to their online work.

Copyrighted work often has a © symbol or the words *copyright by*, to show that you cannot simply copy and share it. Even without a copyright mark, works created by others cannot legally be shared, even if that work appears to be freely available online. Unless, that is, the creator gives explicit permission for the online work to be distributed, remixed, adapted, and/or built upon. A creator can choose to apply one of several kinds of Creative Commons licenses to his/her online work in order to share it. Each license describes exactly how the work can be used legally by others.

The Creative Commons website (http://creativecommons.org) describes six types of license currently in use; each license has a logo that creators can easily add to their work, so that others wishing to use the work know exactly what license permissions apply. Most content creators like to have their work attributed to them, so attribution is a part of all six Creative Commons licenses. There are three additional types of permission embodied in Creative Commons licenses:

- Creators can choose whether they are happy to have the work distributed, remixed, adapted or built upon for commercial and/or non-commercial purposes.
- Creators can decide whether *share-alike* applies – that is, new versions of the work need to have the same license conditions applied.
- Creators can decide whether no derivatives (changed or remixed versions of the work) are allowed.

These three types of permissions are combined in various ways in the six Creative Commons licenses, allowing creators to set the level of protection they desire on their work.

Understanding the basics of online copyright and Creative Commons, and respecting these, is an essential part of being a digitally literate and responsible citizen. Teachers and learners thus need to respect copyright in the use of images and other media. How? You can easily find Creative Commons images to use and attribute in your worksheets on websites like Unsplash (https://unsplash.com/), or images and videos on Pixabay (https://pixabay.com/), or music on dig.ccMixter (http://dig.ccmixter.org/); learners can use these websites to find multimedia for their own digital project work, **blog** posts and PowerPoint slides. You can also show your learners how to search for Creative Commons images in Google by using the advanced search feature in settings, and filtering search results for "Creative Commons licenses".

Here are four examples of good online copyright practices by teachers and learners, that I've seen over the years:

1. Creating a worksheet. A teacher created a vocabulary worksheet for young learners with images of fruit and vegetables. The teacher used a website with Creative Commons licensed images, and attributed each image as required, on the worksheet.

2. Creating online materials. A school creating online materials in a **VLE** wanted to integrate a language quiz that was freely available on another website. The school emailed the website owner, and got permission to link to the quiz on the original website, attributing the site within their VLE. This way learners were able to take the quiz at source.

3. Writing a blog post. A learner wrote a blog post about endangered animals for homework. She carried out a Creative Commons search to find photos of the animals to include in her blog post, and she attributed each image correctly in the post itself.

4. Creating a PowerPoint presentation. A learner created a PowerPoint presentation about her favourite sports, and included a background music clip from the dig.ccMixter website, and two short video clips from Pixabay. She attributed the multimedia and included the Creative Commons license logo for each, on the relevant slides.

Online, a world of knowledge and content is just a mouse click, finger tap or swipe away. Plagiarism has always existed, but many teachers feel that the internet has made plagiarism much easier – and more tempting – for learners.

Plagiarism means taking another person's work, and pretending that it is your own. Teachers often tell me how some of their learners think it's perfectly acceptable to copy and paste whole paragraphs, or even entire essays, from the internet, and to then hand these in as their own work. Most of us agree that verbatim copying of content from the internet, and pretending that it is your own work, is plagiarism, and that this is unacceptable. Our learners need to understand this, and to understand that there can be serious consequences to plagiarism, such as being expelled from a university course, or losing your job.

Plagiarism tools can help us spot plagiarised work, and they can provide evidence of where content has been copied from, by taking us to the source. You can find plagiarism tools online by using a search term like "plagiarism checker". Some plagiarism checkers are free, while others need to be paid for. Many teachers simply copy and paste a suspect text into Google. If the text already exists on a web page somewhere, it's possible that Google will find it for you, so this is a good place to start.

Plagiarism is a complex area. What if our learners reproduce other people's ideas in their own words, but don't say where the ideas come from? Is this plagiarism? Interestingly, teachers can be ambivalent about whether the unattributed paraphrasing of someone else's work is really plagiarism. Plagiarism can mean different things to both learners and teachers. In this scenario, the important thing for learners to understand is the difference between attributing ideas and work to others (that is, quoting your sources), and pretending that the work is your own (plagiarism). In other words, learners need to understand that plagiarism doesn't only mean copying content verbatim. It can also mean not attributing sources correctly. A survey of 879 secondary and high school teachers identified ten common forms of plagiarism, some more serious than others (Turnitin, 2012). They include verbatim copying from a single source, copying from multiple sources, rephrasing sources with no attribution, and recycling one's own previous work with no attribution, among others.

The direct copying and pasting of others' work is, of course, the easiest form of plagiarism to spot. Some teachers tell me that their learners think it's fine to plagiarise if they can get away with it! Whether they do so deliberately or not, it's a good idea to discuss plagiarism overtly with our learners. Depending on their age, they may not have learned that plagiarism is unacceptable. Sometimes learners have been using sources like Wikipedia since primary or secondary school, and nobody has ever explicitly told them not to copy directly from these sites. Often they have not been taught how to attribute or reference their online sources correctly. So we should start by sensitising our learners to the issue of plagiarism. Here's an idea for how to do this. Share the ten most common forms of plagiarism with your learners (see the Turnitin survey website below). Put your learners into small groups and ask them to rate each form of plagiarism on a scale of 1 to 5, to show how serious they think it is (1 = least serious; 5 = most serious). Discuss with the whole class what rating they gave each form of plagiarism and why. Extend the discussion to include how to avoid plagiarism, how to ethically use online sources, and how to reference online sources correctly. You can ask your learners to search online for "how to cite online sources" if this is new to them.

Turnitin (2012). *The plagiarism spectrum. Instructor insights into 10 types of plagiarism.* White Paper. Available at: https://www.turnitin.com/infographics/the-plagiarism-spectrum

> An *ePortfolio* (short for *electronic portfolio*) is a digital space in which learners can store and showcase their work. Teachers and trainers can also keep ePortfolios as part of their continual professional development or to share publicly.

It's useful to divide ePortfolios into three main types.

- A *learning* portfolio reflects development over time and is used to showcase progress.
- An *assessment* portfolio is used for evaluation and may be included as an obligatory part of a language or teacher training course.
- A *professional* portfolio functions as a public CV, showcasing achievements.

English language teachers tend to favour using learning and/or assessment portfolios with their learners. Learning portfolios are especially popular with younger learners and teenagers when there is no pressure of evaluation.

There are no hard and fast rules about what should go into an ePortfolio, because this will depend on its purpose. If a learning or assessment portfolio is part of a formal course, the learner is likely to be told what to store in their ePortfolio. If the aim of an ePortfolio is to provide evidence of language development, content might include essays, PowerPoint presentations, online posters, multimedia projects, and/or audio or video recordings produced during the course. Of course when learning ePortfolios are used for assessment, learners need to be told in advance what criteria will be used to evaluate their work.

Making ePortfolios work with your language learners requires careful planning. The following steps can help:

1. First consider your *objectives* and whether to use a learning or assessment ePortfolio with your learners.

2. Next, consider the *timeframe* and how long you want your learners to keep an ePortfolio. Most teachers plan for their learners to use a portfolio for at least a term/semester, or preferably for an academic year.

3. Decide what digital *content* your learners will need to create and store in their ePortfolios. You could allow your learners some choice in what content they create for their ePortfolios. Map the content to your course plan for the term/year, and share it with your learners, so you all have a clear overview of the digital content to be produced.

4. Choose the most appropriate online *tool* for your learners to keep their ePortfolios. Your institution may already use an ePortfolio tool like Mahara (https://mahara.org/), but if not, your learners could store their work in a Google drive or Dropbox folder, in a **blog**, or in a **wiki**.

5. If you've chosen an assessment ePortfolio, plan how *evaluation* will fit with any other assessment procedures you need to follow (e.g. assignments, tests or exams), and what your assessment criteria are for each of the ePortfolio contents. You may want to negotiate some or all of these criteria with your learners. Also plan in advance how you will give your learners *feedback* on their portfolio work, and how often.

6. Consider how to encourage your learners to *collaborate* on their ePortfolio content. Collaboration can mean learners working together in pairs or small groups on a single **digital artefact,** and it can mean providing feedback and/or peer-assessment on each other's work. Some teachers even work with group rather than individual ePortfolios to ensure collaboration.

7. Finally, think about *audience* by planning who will have access to your learners' ePortfolios. Will it just be the teacher who reviews the portfolio content, or will class members be able to access and view each other's work? For young learners, you may want parents to be able to access and review their child's portfolio work.

Whatever age group you teach or context you work in, planning your use of ePortfolios around these key considerations (*objectives, timeframe, content, tool, evaluation and feedback, collaboration* and *audience*) should help ensure that they are as effective as possible.

E: Tools and trends

Learning technology tools may come and go, but certain types of tools – and certain technology trends – endure. Tools like interactive whiteboards, and trends like the integration of artificial intelligence into learning and teaching, are likely to be with us for the foreseeable future.

38 Interactive whiteboards

Interactive whiteboards began to appear in English language classrooms in the early 2000s, and soon became the latest must-have technology for schools. For teachers to use IWBs effectively, they need to get to grips with both the technological and pedagogical features of this tool.

The term *interactive whiteboard* (or **IWB** for short) is fairly self-descriptive. It's a white-coloured board that is usually mounted at the front of the class. It's connected to a projector and computer, and is touch sensitive, which means that elements projected onto the board can be moved around with a finger or with an electronic pen – this is where the *interactive* part of the term comes from. It's easier to see an IWB in action than to describe it, so if you've never seen or used one, do an online search for "interactive whiteboard" to find a video of one in action. IWBs tend to be expensive, which means they are usually found in high resource contexts.

IWBs are commonly used in two main ways: 1) to bring the internet into the classroom, e.g. by sharing videos, images or other online resources in class; and 2) to share coursebook or teacher-made IWB materials, created on IWB slides (referred to as *flipcharts* in some makes of IWB). Most IWBs have a range of tools, such as a 'spotlight' and/or 'reveal' tool that enables teachers to show only a portion of an image or text at a time, and a 'snapshot' tool that can save board work. Another popular feature of IWBs are interactive transcripts for coursebook multimedia: a transcript can be projected onto the IWB, and when a sentence is touched (with a finger or e-pen), that piece of audio automatically plays. This can be useful for replaying sections of a listening text, for example, to help learners focus on pronunciation features. The interactive nature of IWBs means that learners, too, can come up to the board and move elements around or write or draw on items on the board. Learners' work on the IWB can also be saved and emailed to them or revisited in a future class.

Whether IWBs automatically enhance learning is a moot point. However, over the years I've had the privilege of observing some excellent language learning lessons in which teachers used IWBs very effectively, with learners clearly engaged in and enjoying the lesson. Despite scant research proving a causal link between IWBs and increased learning, many teachers and learners enjoy using them, and report increased motivation in class when the IWBs are used well. For schools that have already invested in IWBs, this is good news. The key to the effective and engaging use of IWBs comes down to teacher training in two key areas: technology and pedagogy. On the technology side, teachers need to gain confidence in using the IWB and its various interactive tools, as well as to know how to deal with technical issues such as calibrating (configuring) the IWB, and this takes practice.

Calibration ensures that the computer that is connected to the IWB recognises where the e-pen (or your finger) touches the board and can accurately work with the IWB software; calibration usually involves touching the whiteboard at several predetermined points during the set up process. Teachers also need to learn how to use IWB software to create their own IWB materials. On the pedagogy side, teachers need to know how to use the technology to create engaging lessons that support what we know about language learning – lessons need to include some input and some language practice (output), for example, as well as regular skills work. Research shows that the two main challenges with IWBs are technical issues, and the tendency for teachers to use them as teacher-fronted tools without involving learners in the use of the board. Knowing this beforehand can help schools set up internal IWB teacher development/training workshops that address these issues from the outset, providing teachers with the confidence and know-how to deal with the technology and the pedagogy of IWBs.

39 Learning platforms

Delivering online or blended courses and classes requires some sort of learning platform, where digital materials can be stored, and where learners can interact with these materials, each other and the teacher.

Learning platform is an umbrella term for the place where we house the digital tools and materials used to deliver online learning. There are a wide range of learning platforms available to teachers, some free and some not. The most complete and complex platforms are usually referred to as **virtual learning environments** (**VLE**s) or **learning management systems** (**LMSs**). Well-known VLEs include Moodle, Canvas, Brightspace and Blackboard. A VLE typically enables a teacher to create their own online course from scratch, by adding content (in the form of multimedia resources), tools for promoting interaction, communication and collaboration (such as discussion forums, messaging features, **wikis** and **blogs**), and tools for creating activities for evaluation (such as quizzes and assignments). In addition to providing tools for content, communication and evaluation, a VLE will include learner grading and tracking – it is this latter feature that makes a VLE one of the most complete learning platform options. A VLE enables teachers to consult logs and reports for individual learners and for the whole class. Logs show participation metrics (such as when learners log in and out, how often and for how long they view specific activities, which activities they've completed or not), and many VLEs issue automated warnings to teachers (and/or learners) when they are inactive for a specified period, or are falling behind in completing tasks. Reports can be generated to show all of this, and also for an individual learner's grades over the course, as well as comparative grades for the whole class. Search online for "(VLE name) gradebook" for more on what grading options are offered by specific VLEs.

VLEs are fairly complex platforms, and are most often used by institutions who will have the IT capability to take care of the technical maintenance of the platform, enrol learners, set up courses – and sometimes even design courses for teachers. There are many alternatives to a full-blown VLE that can appeal more to individual teachers or to smaller institutions. One popular free platform is Edmodo, which contains many of the key elements of a VLE (tools for storing content, for promoting collaboration, and for evaluation) as well as a gradebook feature. Edmodo has fewer learner tracking, grading and reporting features than a full VLE, and it doesn't provide flexibility for course layout and design, but for these very reasons it can be easier for teachers and learners to use. Google Classroom is another popular alternative; again, it is not a full VLE, but it offers many VLE-like features for teachers, and is relatively straightforward to set up and use if you have a Google account (search online for "how to use Google Classroom"). If you or your school are wondering what features the various VLEs offer and which would be best for your needs, search online for "(VLE name) and (VLE name) comparison".

VLEs provide virtual space for mainly asynchronous work, and are often used in tandem with synchronous learning tools, such as instant messaging and video-conferencing platforms. These tools are learning platforms in their own right, and are sometimes used by teachers individually or together for their online or blended classes. Popular instant messaging apps currently include WhatsApp and Telegram, and well-known video-conferencing platforms include Zoom, Microsoft Teams, Google Meet and Skype.

As with any digital technology, there is no single best choice when it comes to a learning platform. The platform or tool you decide to use to support your online or blended course or classes depends on the aims of your course, your and your learners' needs, the technology context (e.g. whether you are working in a high or low resource context), and the other factors explored in 4.

40 Artificial intelligence

Artificial intelligence (AI) has been an integral part of computer-assisted language learning (CALL) for decades. With the increased integration of learning technologies in ELT, AI can be seen in a number of areas. Let's examine some of them.

When I decided to improve my French a few years ago, I downloaded a popular language learning app to see if it would help. Unsure of my level (I'd studied French at school, and then on and off for years), I took the automated placement test offered by the app. Starting with simple items in a multiple choice format, the app offered me items of increasing, similar or less difficulty, depending on whether I answered correctly or incorrectly. After 30 or so items, the app announced that I should look at the learning content for intermediate level. This was my first brush with adaptive testing, and an example of how AI is being used in language learning. Simply put, an algorithm was learning how to read my outputs and adjusting its inputs accordingly. It was behaving intelligently. Of course, the limitation is that the algorithm conceptualises knowing a language as the ability to recognise grammar and lexis. In fact, my French comprehension is high (I can easily understand the radio or newspaper), but my spoken French is much weaker, and my written French is dreadful. This kind of jagged profile for a language learner is typical, but it was not reflected by my app's adaptive test. There are more sophisticated examples of AI in computer-based testing, such as automated writing evaluation (AWE), and speech recognition for oral production, although there are issues with these tools, (see 27); these tools are arguably better suited to formative writing and speaking activities than to summative assessment, at least at present.

Another interesting use of AI in ELT involves using chatbots for language practice. Chatbots are computer programs that simulate human conversation, in written and/or spoken form. The key question for us is whether chatbots help learners improve their English. Research shows that interacting with chatbots can increase low-proficiency learners' confidence with speaking (see the reference below). In addition, some learners find chatbots useful for structured language practice outside of class, although they tend to prefer human-to-human interaction given the choice. In other words, when learners view chatbots as a *supplementary* language learning tool that can increase their exposure to English pronunciation, grammar and vocabulary, the response (at lower levels) can be positive. Nevertheless, chatbots are far from perfect language partners. They often go off topic, make grammar mistakes, and are unable to hold meaningful conversations for long. What's more, the novelty factor of interacting with a chatbot can quickly wear off. In short, interacting with chatbots can support some lower proficiency learners in some contexts some of the time. Some learners seem to find chatbots helpful, at least in the short term, while other learners find chatbots frustratingly limited.

What does this mean for teachers? Learners' reactions to chatbots vary, so you could consider encouraging your learners to try out free chatbot apps and decide for themselves. For example, suggest language learning apps that include chatbots (e.g. Supiki or Mondly) with your low proficiency learners, and encourage them to use an app outside of class for a week or two. Then ask your learners about their experiences and whether they found interacting with a chatbot useful or not. Your learners' interest in interacting with a chatbot is likely to wane over time, but providing extra exposure to language for learners outside of class time is arguably worth attempting – and some learners may be encouraged to continue supplementing their learning outside of class time with a chatbot or other language learning apps.

Fryer, L. K. and Carpenter, R. (2006). 'Bots as language learning tools', *Language Learning and Technology*, 10, 8–14.

> Automated (or machine) translation software translates written or spoken text from one language to another in real time. Is this the technology that has the potential to replace teachers?

First, how does automated translation work? You type a word, sentence or paragraph in one language into a text box, choose the language you want the text translated to, and it appears in that language, instantly translated. Automated translation software can also translate a document, image with text, handwriting, and even the spoken word, from one language to another. One of the best-known automated translation programs is Google Translate, but searching for "translation" in your app store will give you several others to try out. Automated translation apps can be extremely useful for travelling; they can help you communicate in transactional contexts, such as in a taxi or shop, or translate texts, such as a restaurant menu or sign, into a language you understand.

Automated speech translation seems to speak directly to the fear that many teachers have of being replaced by machines. If, say, an Italian businessperson can hold a meeting with a Korean businessperson, with each speaking his or her own language, with everything they say being translated in real time, do they really need to learn a language? Despite increasingly sophisticated programs, automated translation doesn't always get it right. Automated translation is good for common and formulaic phrases, but it is less able to accurately translate nuances in meaning. There is currently no reliable replacement for either a human translator, or for learning to speak a foreign language well, when it comes to *pragmatics*. Pragmatics is the way that language use is sensitive to context: for example, allowing speakers to say less than they mean because the context does the rest. Pragmatics also determines such context-sensitive choices as politeness, sarcasm and humour – choices that translation software is poorly equipped to handle. But automated speech translators certainly come a very close second best, will continue to improve in accuracy and are undeniably useful.

Learners have been using automated text translation for years. Who hasn't received written work from a learner that hasn't obviously been run through Google Translate (or similar), before being handed in as the learners' own work? Rather than trying to persuade learners not to use these programs, or pretending they don't exist, teachers need to see them as a tool that learners will inevitably turn to at times. As such, we can help our learners become critical users of automated translators.

Using automated text translators as bad models is one way to raise awareness of their limitations. For higher level learners, you can give your learners automated translations of texts from their first language into English and, in pairs, get them to identify any errors, and to correct or improve the English translation. For lower levels, it's important to first sensitise students to how unreliable automated translation can be – and how obvious it can be when they use it for their own written work in English! Start with a reverse translation activity. Translate a short English text (e.g. from your coursebook) into your learners' first language through an automated translator, and ask them to identify the weaknesses. By working with a bad model in their *first* language, learners can quickly get a feel for how strange machine translated text can sound, even if the grammar is correct.

'Two-way translation' is another popular awareness raising activity. Take the reverse translated text described above (and which is now in the learners' first language) and use the automated translation program to translate it back into English. Ask your learners to compare any differences between the original English text, and the final version. This can help learners understand that automated text translators are not completely reliable and that, even if they use them, they should be prepared to do some follow-up fine-tuning.

42   Virtual reality

> Virtual reality (VR) is a 3D digital reality that is accessed through a special headset; it is a fully immersive experience that transports you to another world or environment.

Imagine yourself standing underwater on the deck of an old shipwreck, watching tropical fish swim around you and listening to the pull of the tide on the sand. You catch a flash of movement out of the corner of your eye, turn your head, and an enormous whale looms into view, passing by right next to you, its eye level to yours. You could reach out and touch it. As it turns away, the huge back tail flips right towards you, and you instinctively duck. It's such a shock that you pull off your diving helmet – and find yourself standing in a classroom, with a headset in your hand. This was my first experience of virtual reality, and it was extraordinarily real. I clearly remember the experience and the emotions it provoked, even though it took place several years ago.

And herein lies the power of virtual reality, or VR. As a fully immersive experience involving sight and sound via a headset (and with haptic sensors, the possibility of touch and movement), a VR experience can be memorable and meaningful. Research shows, for example, that the immersive properties of VR can help learners to create deep connections with content by blocking out external classroom distractions. VR has been used in vocational training, in fields such as law enforcement, psychology and medicine, for a number of years. VR has also been used in mainstream schooling. For example, primary school learners in Ireland visited a local historical site, then built their own replica of it in a virtual world, which they then explored with Oculus Rift VR headsets (see http://goo.gl/Pi4Lsx for an account of this project). Within the field of ELT, early adopter English language teachers have used VR in innovative ways with their learners, for example as a springboard for task-based learning (see https://ltsig.iatefl.org/tag/virtual-reality/). Some companies deliver VR-based experiences that offer immersive role play scenarios for English language learners, although these companies tend to come and go. ELT publishers too have explored possible uses of VR in English language learning. Cambridge University Press, for example, produced a VR experience of the Cambridge First speaking examination (https://youtu.be/9FQ3hcpM5_I).

Despite its successful use in vocational training, VR has not gained traction widely within ELT, despite some initial interest and ongoing experimentation by teachers and schools. There are several reasons for this. High quality headsets (such as the Oculus Rift or HTC Vive) are expensive, and although much cheaper alternatives exist (such as Google Cardboard), learners still need smartphones and headphones to use VR. Apart from the technology needs, immediate applications of VR for English language learning are less obvious than with other mixed reality technologies, such as AR (see **43**). Because VR transports the user into another reality, physical movement is restricted – the user needs to either stand in one place or sit down. VR is also at heart an individual experience, so learners cannot easily interact with others while they are within a VR setting. Creative EFL teachers have used VR experiences in class as springboards for subsequent sharing and discussion, of course, where learners describe what they have seen and learned in a VR environment. However, given the challenges of providing learners with immediately applicable English language VR experiences in the classroom, VR is likely to remain a technology that appeals to some teachers, and to vocational trainers, and be used occasionally; it is unlikely to become as mainstream as some of the other technologies we've examined in this book. Nevertheless, it remains an option for teachers interested in trying out what can be an emotionally impactful and visually rich technology with their learners.

43   Augmented reality

> It can be useful to think of augmented reality (AR) as
> sitting on a continuum with the real world at one end,
> and fully virtual experiences such as VR at the other end.
> On such a 'virtuality continuum', augmented reality sits
> somewhere in the middle, as it overlays virtual elements
> onto the real world.

AR apps work by opening the camera on a mobile device, and then
overlaying virtual information or objects onto the real world; these
virtual objects appear through the camera lens. Language learning
initiatives involving AR can be dated back to 2011 and earlier, but
AR was – very literally – put on the map of public consciousness in
2016, with the launch of Nintendo's mobile app game Pokémon Go;
within six months it had had over 500 million downloads. In the case
of Pokémon Go, the user's geographical location acts as a trigger to
provide the virtual overlay. Apart from *location-based* AR apps like
Pokémon Go, there are also *marker-based* AR apps, which use a static
image to trigger a virtual overlay, and *markerless* AR apps, which use
the shape of a real object to trigger the virtual overlay.

The use of AR in language teaching is unlikely to ever experience the
sort of uptake and success seen in the world of commercial digital
games, but there have nevertheless been some interesting initiatives. One
early example is the 2011 Mentira project which used an AR location-
based game to teach Spanish in the USA. The project involved learners
taking part in an AR murder-mystery game that required them to collect
evidence in teams by interacting with local residents in Spanish, in a
Spanish-speaking neighbourhood of their city (see www.mentira.org).
Other location-based AR projects have involved university students
creating or taking part in AR university campus tours.

Marker-based AR is also used in English language teaching, mostly on an ad hoc basis by individual teachers looking to experiment with mobile-based learning technologies. My favourite marker-based AR activities involve learners creating their *own* AR content, based on a marker. One example is a gallery walk, where learners (individually or in pairs) choose a famous painting, research it, and then produce an audio guide to the painting, including information such as who it was painted by, when, why, and giving background information about the painting itself. A free AR app like Aurasma can then be used to link a digital image of the painting (the marker or trigger) to each learner's audio recording. Images of each painting are then printed out and put on the walls of the classroom. Using a digital device with the AR app (to read the trigger image), and a headset (to listen to each audio guide), learners walk around the classroom listening to the information about each painting, and taking notes. Learners then work in pairs to compare their notes, and finally the teacher holds a class discussion to check what the learners found out about the paintings, which ones they liked best, and so on. An activity like this could be carried out in print format only – that is, learners research and write paragraphs about a series of paintings; however, the opportunities afforded by AR, where an image and audio (or video) can be linked, arguably create a more engaging **multimodal** experience for learners. For homework, learners can write a short paragraph about which painting they liked best and why. This activity could be adapted so that learners create audio reviews of their favourite book. An image of the book cover functions as the AR marker. Learners use an AR app to read the cover and listen to the reviews. A discussion about which books learners would like to read and why rounds up the class.

Milgrim, P., Takemura, H., Utsumi, A. and Kushino, F. (1994). 'Augmented reality: a class of displays on the reality-virtuality continuum', *Proceedings of the SPIE Telemanipulator and Telepresence Technologies*, Volume 2351, pp. 282–92. Boston, MA: Event: Photonics for Industrial Applications.

44 Digital game-based learning

> Digital games can engage learners in not just learning content, but also in developing critical thinking and more complex problem-solving skills.

When I ask teachers if they are familiar with digital game-based learning (DGBL), many often say, 'Yes.' They then tell me that their learners often complete online drag and drop grammar activities for homework, or use a vocabulary app to revise new words. However, these are automated activities, rather than digital games. Another game-related term that creates confusion is *gamification*, often misunderstood to mean simply playing a game and awarding points to learners. However, the term refers to the *design* behind a learning experience: gamification may include elements of competition that results in learners winning points or badges, or moving up a level. These sorts of rewards are part of game mechanics, and are linked to the goals and the rules of a game. But gamification also includes other elements that are typical of games, such as meaning, motivation, emotion, cooperation, empowerment and/or unpredictability, to name a few. Gamifying a learning experience is not the same as playing a digital game.

Simply put, not all digital games are created equal. DGBL usually refers to more complex educational games that require some thought and effort – not mechanical language manipulation games such as a drag and drop or fill-in-the-gap activities on a computer or mobile device. As computing power and graphics have developed over the past few decades, so more sophisticated, visually interesting games have appeared for all ages. For example, massive multiplayer online role-playing games (MMORPGs), such as World of Warcraft or Fortnite, are popular with adolescents and adults. There is Animal Jam, a simple cartoon-based digital world for six- to eight-year-olds, or Minecraft, popular with pre-teens and teens. However, not all digital games are based on beautiful graphics and/or imaginary worlds. Interactive fiction is a text-based digital game, in which players make choices based on information delivered in text format. A good example of a text-based educational game is Spent (http://playspent.org/html/), in which one needs to try and survive on a very low income by making choices. The aim of this game is to raise awareness of poverty in the USA.

The potential for well-designed games to support language learning is well documented. For example, some educational games can lead to gains in vocabulary acquisition, as well as support the use of certain communicative strategies, such as information seeking, strategising, socialising, and problem solving. Playing educational digital games in English gives learners the opportunity to engage with and practise the language in meaningful and fun contexts. Taking advantage of this, some ELT publishers offer digital games for children learning English. For example, Pearson's Poptropica is an online game in which the player needs to visit different islands, play online and communicate with others, and resolve a problem by overcoming obstacles or completing tasks. The EFL version of the game includes print books that reinforce language learning.

Many games that are not specifically designed for language learning can also be used effectively with English language learners (see the reference below for many examples). As just one example, Animal Jam is a popular educational game about zoology and ecology, available in English and several other languages, and it can be played with young learners aged six and over. These sorts of games are best regularly played together with the whole class, e.g. for ten minutes at the beginning of a lesson once a week. With the teacher controlling the game from a class computer or mobile device connected to a screen, the class chooses and names an animal together. The animal can then move around the virtual world, meeting and communicating with other animals (via text), learning facts about animals, and playing games and collecting points in the form of 'gems'. The teacher can teach and focus on key vocabulary while playing the games with the class.

Stanley, G. and Mawer, K. (2010). *Digital Play*. Peaslake, Surrey: Delta Publishing.

F: Teacher development

Being a digitally literate teacher means knowing how to use technologies not just with your learners, but also to support your own professional development. It also means having strategies to deal with some of the challenges that come with our increased use of technologies, in both our professional and personal lives.

Being 'tech-savvy' refers to knowing about technology and feeling comfortable around it. However, many teachers report feeling less than confident about using digital technologies with their learners.

Nobody knows everything about all technologies. Far from having an encyclopaedic knowledge of digital technologies, I find it useful to think of being tech-savvy as a state of mind. You just need to know enough about technology to serve your needs. This includes choosing only those tools that are likely to significantly improve the teaching/learning experience (see **16**). At the same time, don't be afraid of experimenting. Many technologies are easier than they look on first acquaintance. Even if you feel you know nothing about digital technologies, you probably use several technologies regularly in your personal life. For example, it's likely that you use email, know how to look for information online, and visit websites. You probably have a mobile phone and use that in a number of ways. You may use social media sites, or instant messaging services, or perhaps you use Google Maps to find your way around. The first step towards feeling more confident with technology is to make a list of the things you know how to do with it. Even the most recalcitrant technophobe is likely to have one or two items on their list!

The second step to becoming more comfortable with technologies is to use tools that you or your learners are already familiar with (let them teach you!). You could start with email, for example, by getting your learners to email you their written homework. Or try a chain story, in which learners build up a story collaboratively via email. You write the first few sentences of a story and send it to the first learner on a list (remember to include the list of learners' names and emails). That learner adds a few sentences to the same story, and then emails it to the next learner on the list. And so on, until the completed story is emailed back to you. Review the complete story in class. Or if you know how to use your mobile phone to take photos, choose an upcoming coursebook topic and ask your learners to take a couple of photos connected to the topic before the next class. You do the same. In the next class, share the photos you took, explaining how and why the photos relate to the topic. Then put your learners in small groups and ask them to do the same with their photos. Finally, ask each group to show and tell the class about any interesting photos that were taken. This simple activity activates topic-related vocabulary, is highly personalised – and it's not technically challenging to do! By starting with simple technologies and activities, you will be able to build up your own confidence with digital technologies over time.

Sometimes schools ask teachers to use tools that they may not feel confident using. I've seen this happen with **IWB**s and with **VLE**s, for example. As a short-term solution, you can ask your learners for help with problems during class. But as a longer-term solution, and as a third step towards becoming more tech-savvy, ask your school to set up short informal weekly training sessions to help less confident teachers like yourself become more confident with any hardware or software you're expected to use on regular basis.

Finally, remember for that any technology issue you have, someone else has had exactly the same problem before you! Just search online for information about your tech issue and follow the advice, which will often include step-by-step instructions, screenshots and/or videos. Or use **crowdsourcing,** by asking your social media contacts for help with a specific technology issue. The key is to remember that you are not the first to face a tech problem, and that the answer is almost certainly available online.

The internet has brought us access to more information than we can possibly ever want or need. How to deal with the vast amounts of online information available to us requires an essential digital skill: *filtering literacy*.

You know the feeling. You start to research a topic online, and find more and more related links that you click on and follow. Soon you find yourself bogged down in all sorts of tangential material, and you seem to have forgotten exactly what it was you were originally researching. In internet jargon, this is known as *WILFing* (an acronym for 'What Was I Looking For?'). Then a feeling of panic sets in as it becomes abundantly clear that you can never possibly read everything there is online about your topic. You are probably familiar yourself with this feeling of being overwhelmed by too much information. This is *information overload*, synonyms for which include *infobesity*, *infoxication*, *information glut*, and my personal favourite – *data smog*. These terms reflect the psychological stress that being exposed to an endless stream of digital information causes us. For many, these feelings are exacerbated by social media. Clearly, we should not only be helping ourselves deal with the possible negative effects of information overload, but as educators we should also help our learners develop the necessary skills and strategies.

According to writer Clay Shirky (2012), 'It's not information overload, it's filter failure.' In other words, the amount of information being pushed your way will only decrease if you put filtering strategies in place. Here are some filtering strategies that work for me.

- Select a limited number of *reliable information sources*. In my case, I follow three official news sources (one app, one online newspaper, and one radio station) to keep up with world news. I read four or five **blogs** and a similar number of websites regularly for professional development, and I spend significantly less time on social media than I did a few years back. This works for me, but of course each individual needs to find their own threshold for filtering.

- Use *time management strategies*, by being mindful about – and possibly limiting – the amount of time you spend online every day (see 7). Spend your screen time on worthwhile and filtered online content, however you define that for yourself.
- Use *personal management tools* to help you organise incoming information. For example, use an app like Evernote, Instapaper, or Pocket, to deal with fast incoming information from a source like Twitter, by saving and exploring links later when you have time. Be selective about links you save permanently.
- Filter your information through *trusted sources*. For example, I follow a couple of educational technology bloggers/researchers who are not from the field of ELT, but are all critical thinkers, and highly respected and knowledgeable in their field; I learn a lot from them.

As we can see, filtering literacy involves receiving smaller amounts of online information while ensuring that the information is as reliable as possible. Filtering literacy is not only important for adults – younger learners and teenagers too need filtering strategies, especially when it comes to social media. Whatever age groups you teach, you could challenge yourself and your learners to try each of the four filtering strategies described above, and to report back on the experience to the class.

Filtering is not without its limitations. There is the tendency to create *filter bubbles* in which we access information from like-minded individuals with very similar views to our own, rather than seeking out alternative views and sources which might widen our perspectives. Being able to identify misinformation and disinformation within filter bubbles is an important part of filtering literacy, and another area worth exploring with learners (see **47**).

Shirky, C. (2012). *How the Internet will (one day) transform government*. Available at: https://www.youtube.com/watch?v=CEN4XNth6lo

False information is nothing new, but the internet has undoubtedly enabled the spread of misinformation both faster and further than in pre-digital times. Knowing how to distinguish fact from fiction online is essential for both ourselves and our learners.

You're no doubt familiar with the term *fake news*, which has become highly politicised. It's often used by people to simply discredit information that they disagree with, regardless of whether that information is factual or not. It can be more helpful to distinguish between *disinformation* and *misinformation* online, than to use the term *fake news*. *Disinformation* is false information that is deliberately created with malicious intent; *misinformation* is also false information, but it is not created to intentionally cause harm. Although most of us are unlikely to have created disinformation online, we may well have passed on misinformation to others, unwittingly thinking that it was true.

Online disinformation and misinformation become most obvious in times of crisis. To take just one example, the COVID-19 pandemic resulted in a surge of medical information being shared via text message, audio and video in social networks. Some of it was based on fact, some was not. In times of global challenges that affect us all, it's especially important that we are able to recognise and stop the spread of false information. The wealth of untrue information online in English provides an opportunity for us to develop our learners' critical thinking and digital literacy skills alongside their language skills. At first blush, this may feel unethical. But our learners will be exposed to false information, especially via social media, whether we like it or not. Arguably it is part of our duty as educators to give our learners the tools to evaluate information, and to develop a critical mindset that does not take everything they read online at face value.

One way to do this is through a reading and research activity with learners. Pick a current topic that has generated controversy in the international news – you can find some excellent examples of current false news and rumours on the Snopes website (https://www.snopes.com), for example. Make a list of true and untrue information that has circulated online about your chosen topic, written in the form of statements. In class, ask your learners if they have received any social media messages about the topic, or read things online about it and if so, what. Then give pairs of learners one of your pre-prepared statements. Give them five minutes to research their statement online, and to decide whether it's true or false. They should keep a list of the websites they visited (i.e. their sources). As feedback, get each pair to first read out their statement. Ask the class to vote on whether they think it's true or false. Then get the pairs to share what they learned, what sources they consulted, and whether their statement is true or false.

It's important to get your learners to reflect on disinformation, and how we can unknowingly help spread it via our social networks. Help your learners spot false information online by reviewing these steps:

1. Stop and think. Does the information elicit an emotional response (e.g. fear, anger, excitement) from you? If so, be suspicious!
2. Check the source. Is it authoritative? Is the information coming from an authoritative source, or is it a reported 'fact' from a friend? If the latter, be suspicious!
3. Does the information look fake? Does it have typos, an unknown logo, or an odd URL ...?
4. If you're not sure whether the information is true, check with authoritative sources such as respected news sites. Check several sources if necessary.
5. If you're still not sure whether it's true, don't pass it along!

By sharing these tips, we can help our learners become more critical and more responsible digital citizens.

Opportunities for English language teachers to develop their technology knowledge and skills online abound.

I've been working with in-service teachers for several decades, specifically looking at how they can integrate learning technologies into their online and/or physical classrooms in a pedagogically sound manner. I find that most practising English language teachers feel confident about the *content* they need to teach (e.g. grammar, vocabulary and skills), and they also feel confident about how to do it (i.e. the *pedagogy*). However, teachers can feel less confident about how to integrate the principled use of learning technologies into their teaching practices. Helping teachers develop their own digital literacies is an important step in developing this confidence. The good news is that teachers can take advantage of a wealth of online opportunities and resources to develop their technology knowledge and skills, often at little or no cost, both formally and informally.

Teachers can easily find formal online training courses in a range of learning technology-related areas to suit their needs. Courses range from product-based courses (such as how to use specific brands of **IWBs**, **VLEs** or other software) to skills-based courses (such as how to teach online, or how to integrate learning technologies into the language classroom); these courses may be offered by technology vendors, publishers, or by universities or other educational institutions. Some online courses are free while others are paid for; some online courses consist of just a few hours' work, while some might involve a time commitment of several weeks or even months. However, not all online training courses are created equal, and courses can be of varying quality. See AQUEDUTO (Association for Quality Education and Training Online https://aqueduto.com/) for quality-assured online training courses aimed at English language teachers.

MOOCs (massive open online courses) are another popular online course option for teachers. MOOCs are usually free, although some offer optional assessment and certification for a fee. To find a MOOC in an area you're interested in, do a **keyword search** on any of the main MOOC platforms: EdX (https://www.edx.org/), Coursera (https://www.coursera.org/) and FutureLearn (https://www.futurelearn.com/).

Some teachers prefer to learn in more informal settings, and here we have plenty of online options. Joining an online group of teachers who have a range of expertise in working with learning technologies is a good place to start. Worth exploring are international teachers' association groups like IATEFL's LTSIG (Learning Technologies Special Interest Group https://ltsig.iatefl.org/) or TESOL's CALLIS (Computer-Assisted Language Learning Interest Section http://bit.ly/35p7XqY). Also worth exploring is the Webheads group, who offer free online teacher development courses in a range of learning technologies, called the Electronic Village Online (EVO http://evosessions.org), in January and February every year. The Webheads also offer informal short 'Learning2gether' online events (http://bit.ly/39jBmE2), open to anyone.

Online conferences and webinars are another option for teachers interested in developing their technology skills. Many ELT publishers offer fully online conferences, as do teachers' association groups and educational institutions; these are often free or low-cost, and frequently include sessions on topics related to learning technologies in English language teaching. One of the best ways to find out about online events is to build up your own **personal learning network** (**PLN**) via a social media tool like Twitter, Facebook or Instagram. Start by following some of the organisations mentioned above, and then follow individuals within those organisations who share or post resources or ideas that you find useful. You will soon start to build up a PLN, and can share links, resources and online event information yourself. Leveraging your PLN for professional development is an important part of network literacy for language teachers; it involves not just using resources provided by others, but sharing these more widely, and contributing your own ideas and resources to the PLN when and as relevant. In this way, a PLN can contribute to a teacher's online reputation and influence, and can also form part of an ePortfolio or online CV (see **37**).

Technology can be used in various ways to support informal teacher-led classroom research as well as more formal research as part of a CPD or degree programme.

Research does not reside only in the hands of academics and researchers. Many teachers carry out informal classroom-based research with their own learners on a regular basis in order to develop and improve their teaching skills, or to gauge whether a new approach or tool is effective. There are many technology tools that you can use to support your classroom research, whatever area of teaching or learning you're interested in exploring, and whatever age group you teach. For example, imagine that you would like to carry out a needs analysis with a new group of learners. You could create a series of questions to explore your learners' needs in a free online survey tool, such as Google Forms or SurveyMonkey. Or imagine that you'd like to analyse short texts that your learners produce in a writing activity, to find out which are the most common words they use. To do this, you can copy and paste their texts into a free word cloud tool such as Tagxedo or WordArt, where the most frequent words in the texts are displayed in the form of a cloud, with the highest frequency words larger than the less frequent words.

Teachers can use technology to research their own intuitions about language too. Let's imagine that you want to check what verbs are most commonly used with the noun *money*, to then teach these verb-noun collocations to your learners. You can consult an online corpus (a large online database of real examples of language) to check. For example, searching the British National Corpus for verb collocates of *money* will give you a list of the most commonly used verbs, in descending order of frequency. In case you're wondering, the top five are: *get/got, make, spend/spent, raise* and *pay*.

You may be interested in sharing classroom research ideas with other teachers, or looking for informal research partners. Posting a message to an online teachers' group or calling on your own **PLN** can help you with this. Sometimes you may simply want some ideas or suggestions from your peers, and you could use your online network to informally **crowdsource** these. As you can see from these examples, there are many ways that technology can help you carry out research more effectively.

Whether you carry out informal or formal research with your learners, you need to consider a number of ethical issues beforehand. If you plan to use any of the digital content produced by your learners during your classroom research, for example, to publish an article in a teachers' magazine or as part of formal research in a degree programme, you need to first get your learners' informed consent; this includes permission to refer to their work while guaranteeing their anonymity in anything you publish or share, however informally.

Let's return to the online needs analysis survey example, given above. Here you need to consider issues such as where the survey data are stored online so that privacy is ensured. You also need to be aware of who has access to the survey data, and what possible ends they might serve (apart from your own research). For example, is the online survey company itself allowed to have access to – and even own – the data? And if so, do your learners know this? In order to check this, start with a close scrutiny of your chosen online research tool's Terms of Service (ToS).

The Association of Internet Researchers (AoIR – https://aoir.org/) provides ethical guidelines for carrying out research online (e.g. the use of online surveys, or carrying out online interviews or focus groups) and for data generated or stored online (e.g. learners' online texts, images, audio or video recordings). The guidelines also refer to archived digital data, such as learner records or demographic information, which you may want to use as part of your formal or informal classroom-based research.

Predicting the future of learning technologies is tricky, but there are a number of trends that are likely to be with us for a while. Let's see how teachers can prepare for the future.

No one could have foreseen how a global event like the COVID-19 pandemic would shift teaching online the world over, in the space of a few short weeks (see **2**). It changed perceptions about online teaching and learning. Most teachers realised that teaching online was possible, and although in many cases not perfect, offering learners online options was better than offering them nothing. It also made governments and institutions aware that future-proofing involves having robust blended and online learning options in place so that learners don't miss out on education completely in times of adversity. The result is that online and blended learning is here to stay, and one way for teachers (and institutions) to prepare for the future is to ensure that they are trained in how to design and deliver effective synchronous and asynchronous online learning. This includes hybrid teaching (see **13**), previously a fairly niche way of teaching, but now expected by many learners, especially in tertiary and adult education.

Being able to teach effectively in a range of online modes is in fact part of a wider set of digital literacy skills that current and future educators need. Developing teachers' and learners' overall digital literacies (see **6**) is an essential part of preparing for the future. From knowing how to engage appropriately in personal and professional online networks, to keeping safe online, to respecting online copyright and avoiding plagiarism, to critically evaluating the truthfulness of information we find online … these are all digital literacy skills that we need now, and will continue to need in a world increasingly mediated by digital technologies.

Learning technologies come and go, and the popularity of certain tools and platforms wax and wane. I find that teachers often feel frustrated when a technology tool that they have spent time learning to use suddenly goes from being free to paid for, or when a tool simply disappears. Technology is constantly changing and developing, so a certain amount of *vapourware* (software and tools that are here today, but gone tomorrow) will always be part of the landscape. So, in the words of educational technologist Howard Rheingold, 'If you want to keep up with anything, it's not about keeping up with the technologies, it's about keeping up with the literacies.'

Although learning technologies come and go, there are certain large-scale technology trends that are with us to stay. In the over two decades that I've been working with technology in ELT, one important technology trend has been the move to mobile. Mobile devices have enabled teachers and learners to bring a powerful tool into the classroom and to integrate that tool into their learning. Bringing mobile devices into the classroom has also brought challenges, such as distraction and the need for classroom management strategies and tools (see **29**); it has also highlighted the need for educational institutions to have robust acceptable use policies (see **31**) in place.

Other trends that are likely to be increasingly important for English language teachers in the future are artificial intelligence (AI) and big data. Many teachers and learners already use AI as part of teaching and learning English – for example, through learner tracking in a VLE (see **39**), through automated writing evaluation tools (see **27**), and through automated translation software (see **41**). We won't be replaced by robot teachers any time soon, but we will find ourselves working with more AI as time goes by. Understanding how best to integrate the AI-based educational tools that will be available in the future, is another way for teachers to prepare for the future; and you could start with some of the tools suggested in this book!

Rheingold, H. in Ellis, J. (2012). *Howard Rheingold on how the five web literacies are becoming essential survival skills.* Available at: https://www.niemanlab.org/2012/05/howard-rheingold-on-how-the-five-web-literacies-are-becoming-essential-survival-skills/

Glossary

Behaviourist approach: an approach to learning that works on the principle of stimulus-response. Stimulus in the form of input leads to learner output (response) through repetition, memorisation and recall.

Blog: a journal or diary stored online and consisting of a series of posts. Blog posts appear in reverse chronological order on the blog page, with the newest posts first.

Crowdsourcing: calling on one's online social network for ideas or suggestions.

Cyberbullying: bullying that takes place through digital communication, e.g. in an online social network, or via SMS text messages or group messaging apps.

Digital artefact: a digital product (e.g. an image, slide, audio, video, meme, etc.) that can be stored or shared online.

Dyslexia: a learning difficulty that makes reading or interpreting letters and words challenging. It does not affect overall intelligence.

Dyspraxia: a developmental disorder that affects movement and coordination.

Feature phone: a simple internet-enabled phone that usually includes camera, audio and video features.

Gamification: the application of game mechanics to learning activities to increase engagement.

Hyperlink: an electronic link in a digital document/web page; clicking on the link enables one to move to another point in the same document or to navigate to another web page.

Interactive whiteboard (IWB): a large digital board connected to a computer and usually placed at the front of the class. Users can touch or write on the board with a digital pen, a keyboard and/or their fingers.

Keyword search: the use of key terms in an internet search engine to find specific content online.

Learning management system (LMS): an online platform or virtual space used to support online learning. LMSs usually include discussion forums; content in the form of uploaded documents, audio and video; and assessment and grading features. Often used interchangeably with the term **VLE**.

Malware: software that is created to damage a computer or to gain illegal access to the computer's contents.

Memes: a humorous text, image or video that is widely shared online, often with slight changes.

MOOC: short for massive open online course. A MOOC may have thousands of learners enrolled at the same time.

Multimodal: a synonym for *multimedia*, that is, any combination of text, image, audio and video.

Personal learning network (PLN): a network of online peers in a social network, individually created by teachers to support their learning or professional development.

Phishing: the practice of sending fraudulent emails or text messages, often with links, in order to steal an individual's financial information or passwords.

Screencasting: using screen capture software to record one's computer screen; an audio or video commentary can be added while recording.

Sexting: sending sexually explicit images or text messages via a mobile phone to another user.

Virtual learning environment (VLE): an online platform or virtual space used to support online learning. VLEs usually include discussion forums; content in the form of uploaded documents, audio and video; and assessment and grading features. Many VLEs also include learner tracking capabilities. Also see **LMS**.

Web 2.0: online sites and apps that enable user-generated content and sharing, such as blogs, podcasts and wikis.

Wiki: a series of editable online pages, created and shared by users.

Index